MLM – Crime Case?

Multi-Level-Marketing,

Network-Marketing,

Direct Sales:

Rip-Off or Business of the 21st Century?

By S. Ralf Carter

Imprint

In case of questions regarding the book's content, feel free to get in touch with the author:

https://www.facebook.com/SRalfCarter/

Table of Content:

Warnings upfront:

You're looking for recommendations, with which specific network-marketing company you should sign up? Sorry, this you won't find here.

You are seeking out horror stories of innocent victims having been screwed by evil organizers of chain letters, and who consequently have lost tons of money? Again sorry, you won't find those in this book, either. Well, maybe you will, but only to a small degree.

Why's that?

Reality produces far less glamorous headlines than the mass media needs to make a living. In media productions, it's not all that uncommon to massage and knead facts until they don't resemble the original items even remotely – as long as it captures the audience, all is fine.

While this attitude may yield crispy headlines and so-called investigative journalism, it doesn't do much for you and me. Even worse, we work ourselves up into a rage due to perceived injustice in our world, and then we demand, "Somebody needs to do something" about it – so we expect that elusive "somebody" to take care of the thinking and doing on our behalf, and we ourselves are none the wiser.

What *can* you find in this book?

Let me answer with three counter-questions:

How does your life look like today?

How will your life look 10 years from now – if you continue doing what you having been doing until now?

Compare the two previous answers and tell me **if that is enough for you**.

Now, please.

Should your response to this last question have been some form of "**yes**", then feel free to stop reading this book right away. There are many seriously good novels in the book market, and almost as many good non-fiction books. Grab something relevant to your preferences and enjoy a pleasant evening with a great book (in case you enjoy serial novels and your mornings tend to find you grumpy, have a look at the Winter-Library by Jane St. John; personally, I love her style of smiling irony – and you may be able to find some sympathies for the main character).

Seriously. If you won't be able to gain additional value from my thoughts in this book, any further reading doesn't make much sense. Save yourself the frustration and simply put this thing down!

Still here?

Well, in this case, I venture out to assume something about the 10-year-forecast from today's perspective didn't find your appreciation.

Admittedly, it won't be too easy for my monologue (called "book") to extract what precisely you didn't like about that outlook. That's even more reason to start right away. Shall we?

What's wrong so far?

I am aware how presumptuous it may appear to talk about somebody I never met in person and I know nothing about (this somebody would be you). Nevertheless, give me a moment to make my point, please. A point derived from personal experience, repeated over and over by yours truly, until the metaphorical penny finally dropped. I'm not the fasted, as I will readily admit.

If your outlook for your life ten years from now didn't please you all too much (which I take the liberty to assume, since you are still reading), then this is usually due to (at least) one item on this short list of reasons:

- Your salary or compensation doesn't show indications of any substantial increase; unfortunately, expenses like rent, utilities and car fuel seem to behave less moderate
- While you can see yourself earning quite a bit more by means of working, this also would take a substantial increase in your work load to make it happen. Ten years from now, you won't be any younger than today – which makes the idea of **even more** work hours sound a bit like a sneak preview of hell
- You current working climate is more burden than pleasure; the prospect of continuing like this for at least another ten years certainly has characteristics of a serious threat
- You are actually doing well and your job or self-employment does provide you with a decent amount of income; however, it puts heavy pressure on your available time, causing your personal life experiences to get the short end of the stick
- You don't have a job, are not self-employed, and you have little hope about anything changing anytime soon, at least not in terms of income. Means: you are on some type of no or fixed income (e.g. government handouts), which doesn't provide for any confidence in your future whatsoever

Am I completely wrong? Ok, maybe in your case my angle is slightly off, but give me some wiggle room – can you at least recognize one of those aspects?

Great – in that case, there is a cure!

The cure for many symptoms

All of the points mentioned on my list are symptoms of the same root cause. A civilization disease, if you will. This root cause we can call "TFM."

TFM?

Yep, TFM is the problem. As you probably have noticed, it happens to be a three-letter-acronym (TLA). Moreover, it stands for a catastrophic concept that we ingested since our earliest childhood. It stands for "Time for Money" – your time for other people's money, that is.

Whenever you want to obtain additional income from your job or profession, for most part it amounts to giving up more of your life's time in exchange for that additional income. That's the infamous "working overtime" or "having a second job," both probably no strangers to many workers, white and blue collar alike.

If the data typist wants more money, she needs to offer up additional hours. Should the dentist feel the need for more income, he has to serve additional patients, hence work more hours. Even the piece-worker, who in theory is paid for additional pieces of work rather than additional time expended, usually ends up flipping life time for the money – simply because the additional work intensity has used up more of his energy reserves, which he will need to replenish at the expense of his spare time.

In my extended family, pretty much everybody has made income decisions based on questions like "is it a full-time job?" or "how much salary per month?"

You can't spell "Time for Money" much clearer than that.

Then how?

Fortunately, there are cases providing us with examples of a different approach. The owner of a store will, hopefully, sooner or later recognize that his income is not directly dependent on the number of hours he spends in his store. Instead, the income is a result of the number of happy and satisfied customers and of the profit margin he can achieve for the products sold. Once the store owner has figured that one out, his thinking will shift from "more hours in the store" to "how do I get more satisfied customers into the store?" Which, in turn, has little to do with the number of hours – and is much closer connected to meaningful utilization of tools like advertising, word-of-mouth, customer recommendation programs, and the like. It's not unheard of to see profits improving because of reduced working hours.

Are you saying I should not work anymore?

You are asking whether I meant to say you should lean back, feel groovy, and just let the day pass by itself? Oh no, that's not what I have said – and don't you dare to claim I did.

What I am trying to say, however, is this: Feel free to start separating in your mind the aspects of income and current workload. Ironically, that's precisely what many of us have done already – just using the wrong sequence:

We spend the money long before we got around to earning it. That's called debt and comes in many shapes and forms: credit card debt, car loans, home mortgage, school loan, or simply "I'll pay you later" (also known as trade credit, although it doesn't matter much whether it comes from a supplier or from a friend).

Whenever we are using debt, we have pulled income from the future into the here and now – by means of so-called creditors. The help of those creditors comes at a price and it's not a low price either: if you simply carry a balance on your credit card for 4 years (not talking about adding debt on top – just rolling the balance forward month over month, paying off only the minimum required amount), then you usually will end up paying **twice** the original amount. This way, the original 800 for the new bed end up morphing into 1600 for a not-so-cozy-bed by the time you finally paid it off. However, those payments dribbled away in smaller slices, so it didn't feel too painful. That's a phenomenon, which you will encounter frequently.

Oh no, I am not raising my index finger and calling you out: I am the very last person entitled to such behavior, rest assured. I myself have made that very mistake untiringly and in more cases than I care to remember. However, that's precisely why I have earned the right to at least point the issue out to you.

The biggest of all problems are the so-called consumer loans – those are offer by numerous department stores, car dealerships, and banks. Commonly, they are easily obtainable, at least as long as you have a stable job. That by itself should tell you something.

Tomorrow for today

Clearly, it's absolutely legit for banks to try and sell their products – and their main products happen to be loans. However, you aren't forced to buy them (e.g. nobody is forcing you to accept the bank's money).

More specifically, a consumer loan features an interesting problem: there is only one way to get rid of it – specifically, you must pay it off; usually with cash for which you need to work like a slave. So, how exactly do you get the cash to pay off the loan? Well, same approach as already before: you trade your time for money and therefore spend time of your life to get rid of that iron chain. And it's not sufficient to simply pay back the amount you borrowed. Nope, there are those additional interests taking their own sizeable bite out of your life's time.

Now, let me ask you: do the days in your future (say, next year) come with more hours per day?

No? Strange.

Can future years at least provide you with more days per year?

Again no? Very odd...

Then, what makes you believe paying off the loan plus interests in the future would be easier for you than it is today to come up with the amount of money right away without resorting to a loan? Phrased differently: if you can't afford a purchase today (which is why you need the loan, right?), why do you believe you can afford it today with tomorrow's money?

Fact is: if you cannot afford something today, borrowing will make the problem bigger – not smaller.

A slightly different situation we have at our hands if somebody else is paying off the loan for you. If, for example, you borrow money to buy an already-gushing oil well **and** you pay a low enough (!) amount for that well, then the loan might be paid off by the people who are buying the oil from you. Such a loan would not be eating into tomorrow's income but instead may actually produce a surplus after the sales proceeds have taken care of the loan payments. Banks are referring to this type of loans as a "commercial loan." And are far less enthusiastic about these commercial loans than they are about consumer loans. Strange, isn't it?

Obviously, the behaviors of banks are not based in pure evil but in actually meaningful economic considerations. Alas, those considerations reflect the interest of the banks, not necessarily your best interest – which is why we don't need to concern us the banks' reasonings; after all, they didn't pay for this book. So why would we care about the financial institutions here?

Important thing to take home: even if you can obtain a consumer loan, you should not do so. Simple, actually. In theory.

As we progress along the line of this book, we will encounter the question of starting a self-employment without bank loans again later. To be precise: we will encounter, how and why it's actually easier to start without a loan than it is to start with a loan. For that, though, I have to ask for your patience.

Let me recap:

We are quite well able to separate our current spending from our ability to produce income – with instruments called loans or debt. That way, we can spend today what we are consequently obliged to earn tomorrow or the day thereafter. **Hopefully** earn tomorrow, as I wish to add – nobody possesses the proverbial crystal ball, therefore your tomorrow's ability to earn enough to repay the loan is more hope than it is known fact.

However, you can play the game the other way round as well: You can arrange for income today, which you then will be able to spend in the future.

Today for tomorrow

This method, too, is well known to most of us – but somehow much less appreciated. The best-known incarnation is called "saving": you are working today and putting aside a small fraction of the earned money, usually into some type of savings account with a bank. After a while, you have accumulated enough money that you can use to pay for fulfilling your wishes and desires – in which case you take the saved money, spend it on whatever you want to buy, and continue to save for the next purchase. This way, your money continues to piles up because you don't have to use your cash to pay off old debt – which makes it the opposite of a loan.

Frequently, saving money is somewhat ridiculed with the trivial hint "You can't collect any decent interests for savings nowadays. Why save?"

The answer should be fairly obvious: by saving, you are able to spend your own money for your purchases without having to burden your future with the consequences. Whether or not you collect any interests for the saved amount, that fact is at best marginal – the important aspect is the lack of interest payments you need to make to the bank for years to come (as would be the case with a loan). **Those are the really important interests in this equation – the ones not paid.**

The problem surrounding the process of saving money happens to be the mentality, which has been hammered into our heads for decades: you can have today what you can afford not before the day after tomorrow. Why wait? Instant gratification.

Saving is a slow process, but in turn it is extremely simple. Even simple enough for a bank to understand it – you can issue the order to automatically transfer a part of your salary to your savings account every time you are paid. That way, the bank takes care of the work and you reap the benefits. Start out with very small amounts and increase them over time.

In fact, the amounts can and should be so small and occur so frequently, that you won't notice them disappearing. Unfortunately, banks tend to burden you with high costs for the transfers, which is kind of defeating the purpose: if you transfer 10 Dollar (or whatever your local currency happens to be) and are charged another 2 Dollar for doing so, that would be missing the target, wouldn't it? What can you do in such cases, when dealing with a bank charging more or less high amounts for the mere act of transferring your money?

Somewhat obvious, actually: go and find a bank or an account, which is not burdening you with such expenses. There are plenty of banks offering accounts for a monthly fixed fee (or even free), in which cases it doesn't matter how many individual transfers you are executing.

Way back when, I did start saving by transferring 10 Deutschmarks (which discloses my age a bit) to a building society savings account, weekly and fully automatic. Since it was quite difficult to get my hands on the money in that account, this was my way of making sure I don't get my greedy hands on it "accidentally." Neither this savings account nor my checking account did charge a per-transaction fee, so those savings contributions were actually free transactions.

After some months, those (for example) weekly 10-Dollar-transfers have dropped out of your recognition and consequently don't hurt you anymore. At that time, you increase this continuous savings contribution a little bit. How much this "little bit" will be, that depends a good deal on your personal circumstances – for some, it might be 12 instead of 10. For others, it may mean 100. It doesn't matter – just make sure it is more than it was before.

Then, you continue saving that new amount on a (preferably) weekly base. Until you don't notice this amount disappearing from your account, at which time you go back and increase the savings contribution by another bit. And so on.

That sounds like a ridiculous strategy? It is. However, it's precisely the strategy applied by all those countless subscriptions for magazines, internet web site memberships, pay-tv and last, but not least, the government's payroll taxes: reliably recurring withdrawals from our account or salary will be accepted into our mind as "given fact", so we will make work with whatever is left over. This automatic self-limitation is a phenomenon well known by anybody who wants to help him- or herself to your money. Why don't you utilize it yourself to accumulate money for your own benefit, for a change? That way, you can pile up savings without feeling the pain of not having the money to spend.

Sow and harvest

Another variation of the "earn today and spend tomorrow" is income, derived from today's work but which will flow to you at a later time.

Don't get me wrong, I am not talking about salaries simply being paid too late (that wouldn't be too hot). Instead, I am referring to a different kind of income – which brings us right to the core topic.

When you work for your employer and are paid for doing so, this time-for-money payment covers everything your employer (or client) will ever owe you for this work.

In case the employer turns the fruits of your work into something greater, yielding him a huge chunk of money sometime in the future – that's lucky him. You will not be paid any additional amounts for that work.

On the other hand, should your work project turn out to be a bust for the employer, he can't come back and take away a part of the amount already paid. Sure, he can fire you – but that only means he will not pay you additional amounts for **future** work. Your work from the past has already been paid for, regardless of the economic outcome for the employer.

This, however, may be just the reason why specifically those of us, who are not all that sure whether or not their work is worth the amount they are being paid, are looking for a "safe and secure job." It's those people who regularly demand higher salaries using reasons like minimum wages, comparable wages, industry averages, and "I deserve to get paid the same as everyone else."

Truth being told, you are absolutely worthless for your employer unless you are producing at least what he has to pay for you **and** your workplace (as in: your salary plus associated costs plus government charges for your labor). If you can't generate that much income for the company, it would be inherently stupid to employ you at all. I hope that your employer is not a stupid one – otherwise, you may get paid more than what you are worth, but not for much longer. Economics will put an end to this, for sure.

Those of us, who are aware of their labor's value **and** who know whether this value is substantially higher than what they are getting paid – those people don't have to use phrases like "comparables" or "minimum wage law". Why not? Because they have an entirely different caliber of negotiative ammunition at their disposal: "My skills provide the company with additional income of around $xxx per hour.

I think it's beneficial for the company to pay me a fifth of that amount, so I have the means to further increase the value of my labor for the company."

Improving your value for your employer is certainly an entirely reasonable and lucrative approach to increase your future income – simply because salary continues to flow to you, once you have negotiated the amount (and didn't screw up too badly afterwards). So, improvements today yield income tomorrow and thereafter. Without additional work hours, mind you. Simply by providing better work because it is more informed work.

Exactly how would you know how much your work is worth for your company?

What, you don't know that? What specifically are you doing all day on the job, if you don't know the basic facts? I mean, seriously, if you don't know the business of your employer even this little bit, there might be your problem right away. If you don't care for the business of your company, you shouldn't expect the company to care about you. Or your salary, for that matter.

Might it be that, in your opinion, the company employing you simply is too large and opaque for you to understand it and to employ the figure-out-my-value approach? Well, that may be so. In which case you should ask yourself whether your future is important enough for you to find something else where you **can** determine your value.

I am not suggesting you leave your job and change the company – although maybe that would be an approach, too. However, this certainly isn't the basic idea here.

What you could do, though, is to come up with a type of work "on the side," where you can get closer to the levers of sustainability. Something allowing you to convert today's work into a repeating income stream instead of a one-time payment.

Of course, you could accomplish something like that by collecting the payment for today's work and stuffing it into projects created by somebody else – that's the method banks prefer to sell you under the umbrella term "investment".

As a matter of concept, such an investment is a situation where some-body takes your money and uses it for (hopefully profitable, may your prayers be heard) business endeavors which may or may not yield some income for you in the more or less far future. Along the road, the recommending bank and the organizer of this money pooling scheme as well as the manager of the operation are receiving an ongoing com-pensation for their involvement. The only one at the table who is not granted a steady and guaranteed income stream happens to be you. In other words: for a very long time, you are paying for the investment bank, the organizer, and the manager. Of all people, those are the three groups of which each has way more money than you do. Can you spot the problem?

Exactly – the incentive for those groups to work hard for the project's success is mediocre at best. They are paid even when there is no suc-cess at all. You, however, are the one left holding the proverbial bag.

The fact that along each step of those transactions your local incar-nation of the vampires of bureaucracy (aka governments, in all their manifestations) are siphoning off substantial parts of your money, this fact shall be mentioned only for reasons of completeness: if you're gainfully employed today, payroll taxes and social insurance contri-butions easily gobble up half of your labor's compensation (most of that large amount you don't see, and that's intentional. Today's gov-ernments have learnt to divvy up their grabs for your money into many smaller chunks, and a good part of those grabs doesn't even bear their name – so you don't immediately see what's going on. You may despise them for it, or you may approve of it – but either way, they at least could be honest and use the correct name for what they are doing, specifically "taxes" instead of "contributions", "unemploy-ment insurance", "social insurance", "disability insurance", "social burden sharing" and so on. Even if a large part of those payments has to be paid by the employer, from what did you expect the company to pay those amounts? From the compensation for your labor value, of course – leaving less for you.)

With the remaining half, you are encouraged to first pay the banks, insurances, broker, initiators, managers, and all the others – who surely provide valuable services. The question simply is: are those services for your small amounts of money valuable enough to justify spending the investment returns of years or decades for them? Frequently not, I would assume; but that's something you have to decide for yourself.

To wrap it up, you would be looking for something where you can/need to contribute today's work and will be paid for it later; those payments should then continue for a longer period of time, preferably for the rest of your life. Not necessarily every month the same amount (there are no straight lines in the universe and nothing is perfect, though one can wish), but as a basic goal that doesn't sound all that bad, does it?

Geese and golden eggs, cows and woolmilkpork

What might be the reason for you getting so much less for your work than it may ultimately turn out to be worth? The answer can be found in uncertainty of the future.

Nobody, not even you, can know today what the future will actually look like. Oh sure, we have a pretty good expectation, a rough idea, of what should be probable. But **know** we do not.

This uncertainty is taking that huge bite out of your salary (or your fee, if you are self-employed). As mentioned before, employers and clients cannot come back after the fact and take away part of the payment simply because their business project as a whole didn't pan out the way they had hoped for. Thus, they need to adjust your compensation upfront, based on statistics or (more likely and less accurate) heuristics, i.e. gut feeling.

How do you calculate the future? I don't intend to get ourselves into the bone-dry details, but let me say as much: there is an entire industry dealing with precisely that question, namely the insurance industry. Looking at the large sums of money piling up at insurance companies, it seems pretty obvious that the ultimate solution amounts to them keeping more of your money for their own pockets, just to be on the safe side.

That's how insurance underwriters are operating, that's how banks are operating, and that's how employers are doing it with regard to the salaries, too. If in doubt (which is almost always the case), it's best to keep more and pay as tiny a wage or salary as is humanly possible.

Which is entirely sensible and reasonable. Again: from their point of view.

That is not necessarily also your point of view, I presume. In this case, there is only one solution to the problem: instead of grudgingly biting this "safety discount" taken by others, you have to absorb this uncertainty yourself. In turn, you will be able to keep more of what you worked for.

Insurance sales people, for instance, are well acquainted with this aspect – think about it: not only are they selling insurance contracts, which in and by themselves are trying to make a profit from swallowing other people's uncertainty about the future. On top of that, the insurance agent on his part suffers a hefty amount of uncertainty with this very contract he just sold to a customer just like you: how on Earth would anybody know at which point in the future you are going to terminate this insurance contract? Since insurance companies are in the business of handling other people's uncertain future (and do so for profit, I might point out), their approach to handling this question should not come as a surprise: oftentimes, the insurance agent has a choice whether to receive a discounted payment right away (this is called "zillmerized", named after the German actuary August Zillmer who invented it), or to receive tiny commission payments on an ongoing base over the lifetime of the insurance contract from which those commissions are derived.

We are probably not surprised to learn that most insurance agents opt for the Zillmer version of getting paid (e.g. give me the money **now**; yeah, it's less, but it's right now). This bias has not gone unnoticed by the insurance companies themselves, obviously. Which is why they have moved to a mixed model, allowing them to claw back part of commissions paid long ago, if and when an insurance contract is terminated earlier than they expected. In other words, now the insurance agents are really screwed. No matter what the outcome might be, the insurance will win one way or the other, while the insurance agent bears the risk even if he opted to accept a lower commission payment as risk mitigation. Means: the insurance sales person always and inevitably will get less than the real value of his work. Oh well, the insurance agent should have known who he is dealing with, right?

And by the way, the default way of dealing with the agents' constantly being taken advantage of by the insurance companies, in turn, for many sales people happens to be the creeping deterioration of their work's value, which is precisely why insurance sales people as a group have such a bad name. This, too, is yet another theme we will encounter later again in a different context.

Apparently, we can't rely too much on changing the compensation model with our employer or client – somehow, they'll manage to bend it to their liking anyway, eventually. It should be obvious that in this context "their liking" implies "**not** your liking."

The appropriate response to this situation most likely is to get out of the unfortunate dependency per se – simply because the question of your future income also happens to be the question about who has more leverage. Who is operating on the longer side of the lever: your contract partner, or yourself?

As long as you are an employee of your contract partner (i.e. employer), your leverage is akin to that of a nail file compared to a pipe wrench. With your side being the nail file, in case that wasn't clear. Weak starting position, to begin with.

That's where self-employed persons stand on a slightly better base, if they have sufficiently many clients (and that's a big if). But if a self-employed software developer has essentially only one client, then he has a boatload of problems – not the least of which being that the client of course can count work hours. As soon as the client is able to determine from simply adding up the hours for the month and figure out easily how important a client he happens to be, then for all intents and purposes, this software developer is an employee of his client. With all consequences of being an employee, such as having almost no pricing power for his work.

I am willing to even go one step further and boldly assert: self-employment is insufficient for your purposes because frequently it's just a different model of TFM. Which improves the situation by not a single iota.

What you really need to aim for, that's the activity of a business owner. Don't fret - the difference between a self-employed and a business owner is merely the mental approach to the problems, nothing else. At least for now and for our purposes.

This small difference in your mental approach will ultimately make all the difference between a hammock in the Caribbean and a bed in a hospital, one of them hosting a relaxed and successful person, the other one a burnt-out victim of the daily rat race.

What does a business owner do?

The Hawaiian-American author and business owner Robert T. Kiyosaki differentiated the types of income sources into four groups, which he presented in a 2x2 matrix:

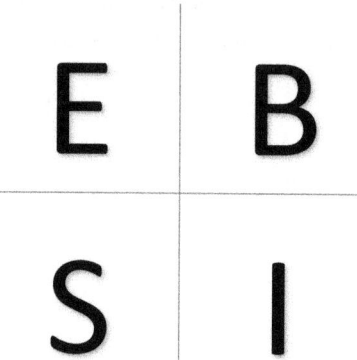

Those four letters are standing for:

E – Employee

S – Self-Employed

B – Business Owner

I – Investor

From Robert Kiyosaki's point of view, employees and self-employeds differ only in terms of the mad person they consider to be their boss. Employees usually have to deal with a head of workgroup, head of department, assistant vice president of their line of business or somebody else they can drag in front of a court, should the need arise (which surprisingly often does arise indeed).

The self-employeds, on the other hand, have an insane psychopath as a boss whom they cannot sue in any court on this planet: themselves.

In both cases, however, they essentially have a job and trade their time for money. For the employed person, there are some laws preventing destructive abuse of the employee. For the self-employed, there are no such laws stopping him from ruining his own health and, soon before or thereafter, his financial situation.

Self-employeds are usually perfectionists, absolutely convinced nobody else is able to perform their work even remotely as good as they themselves can do it. Whether this holds true, however, is a horse of an entirely different color.

The only self-employed persons with a real chance for economic survival are extreme specialists. That is, professionals who you want to hire because of the person, not because you just happened to need somebody providing such service and this guy just happened to be in the area.

If you need brain surgery, you want **the** best, most fanatic brain surgeon you can find – there is no second brain in your head to try another surgeon.

Looking for a bookkeeper? In that case, you are more likely to ask for the costs associated with their work. Because: if the cheapest bookkeeper screws things up, you can still grab your stuff and bring it to the next-lowest-cost competitor to let that person have a shot at it. So, why not start with the cheapest option?

The business owner is somebody who creates a business and then spends most of his working hours on improving that business. Please note: **improving** the business. He won't spend time on improving the product or on doing a better job on a function somebody else is supposed to perform – that's what employees and sub-contractors are for. The purpose of a business owner is similar to the job of a conductor, making the orchestra of employees and contractors work together smoothly and efficiently. That, by the way, happens to be an ongoing task – the world changes quickly; therefore the business has to accommodate those changes. Preferably without losing its efficiency and all the while remaining a place where people enjoy working.

Finally, the last category of income producers is the investor. The Investor and his capital enable other businesses to execute on projects, which they wouldn't have been able to get done without the money provided by the investor.

Key to understanding the investor's work is their search for situations where business skills are present and technical preconditions are all met in the business, as it already exists. Alternatively, at least the prerequisites need to be easily obtainable once the money is available to pay for them. Further, the management of that business must have convincingly demonstrated in the past the ability to orchestrate all necessary production factors, such as people, material, capital, licenses, real estate and so on. If, and only if, those requirements are met **and** capital (money) is the last piece missing, then the investor can step up to the plate and provide that missing capital.

To make meaningful decisions, the investor obviously needs to understand the issues at hand – individually for each individual project. The Investor needs to know the respective type of projects, needs to be able to read and understand financial data of the company, needs to have a well-founded opinion on where the markets will be going while the project is proceeding. After all, how intelligent is an investment in drilling oil wells if you don't have a clue of the demand for oil in that area over the next 5 years (which would be exactly the time at which you need to sell the black goo from precisely those wells)?

Of those 4 quadrants (E, S, B and I) only two have the ability to produce virtually unlimited income for the future without you having to continuously trade time for money; the two are (obviously) business owner and investor.

To start as investor, you need - among many other preconditions - mainly the one commodity you are expected to contribute to projects: capital, frequently in the form of money. Unless you own or have access to large piles of cash not needed elsewhere, there is no point in pursuing the idea of becoming an investor. Before you can act as investor, you need to have sources of income to make and keep you independent (i.e., not depending on the money you intend to hand over to the company, in which you plan to invest).

That leaves your current self with the vastness of available options consisting of exactly one and one only: the business owner. So far, so good.

How do I become a business owner?

This question is not as easy as the ones encountered before. We all have the feeling we should fill out some forms or visit an office of a government entity, in order to become a business owner. Alas, that's not how it works. Because:

Business ownership is a mindset. It's a concept, an idea. The two things in this universe, which you will find neither on forms nor at governmental institutions, are concepts and ideas. So – don't go looking there.

Now, obviously at some point you will have to talk with government bureaucrats or file forms. But those will be consequences of, not the cause for business ownership.

By the way – it has come into fashion to call business owners "entrepreneurs," probably to de-emphasize the ownership aspect of it. I am not sure whether this is a result of strong socialist tendencies in our society (where it is ok to slave away like a mule, but frowned upon to own the resulting benefits) or if it simply tries to point out that "ownership" is not the only operative aspect. Either way, we will not call the business owner "entrepreneur" for the simple reason that the word "entrepreneur" starts with the letter "E" - which is already used for "employee" and therefore not available to Robert Kiyosaki's cashflow quadrant.

You turn into a business owner by thinking and acting like one – not by filling out a business registration or filing Articles of Incorporation with the Secretary of State (or whichever government entity collects the fees for it in your neck of the woods). And no, it's not a joke. I have been asked more than once something along the lines of

"I don't get it. I have incorporated and filed the required documents with the government, I even applied for the business registration. But still nobody is calling my phone or wants to buy anything from me – what has gone wrong?"

Maybe knowledge of some facts might help: in any major country, there are millions of companies with the legal structure of a corporation or limited liability company. On top of that, there are even more businesses operating as partnerships (usually limited partnerships, some unlimited). Add in some more exotic legal structures, commonly found in places where taxation is based on the legal structure (aka Europe) plus the gargantuan number of self-employed professionals and sole proprietors. Potential customers can pick any of those businesses. Exactly what would compel anyone into calling specifically **you**?

Makes for an interesting question, does it not?

Trying to answer this question will lead us deeper into the rabbit hole than many may expect at this point...

What should my business do? What about myself?

It's true, you are not the same as your business, and you should not confuse the two. At some time down the road this will be of importance.

That said, whom are you kidding? Right now, at the very beginning, your business has exactly one employee – who happens to be yourself. Therefore, save your schizophrenia for some later point in time and face the facts: it's just you, yourself and nobody else. And that is a good thing.

Don't believe for a second others wouldn't notice. Regardless of the (in your opinion) impressively sounding title on your business card – or in the signature line of your emails, in case you can't afford the business cards – may it be "Managing Director", "CEO", "President", "Emperor" or whatever else comes into your mind: people notice who they are dealing with. Drop the pretentious stage performance and get down to business; that usually works much better. As long as there are no job descriptions in your business, don't put one on your business card. Yep, those are job descriptions and not status ranks, just in case this aspect escaped your attention. The only information needed on your business card is your name, how to reach you, and what you have to offer. Those pieces of information, however, better should be clearly legible and easy to figure out. What else would be the purpose of a business card?

Purpose of your company?

If your country or municipality requires any type of registration forms (and they usually do, after all they want a part of the money you are making), there is one question which comes up over and over again – and surprisingly often this one question causes serious issues for the freshly baked business owner: what do you write into the field asking for your "business purpose" or "business activity"? Essentially, they are asking for your justification in the business universe, your company's raison d'être.

Sounds innocuous enough, doesn't it? Well, it is. Yet, I have seen many business startups put the uttermost ridiculous words in these form fields, almost as if this question hit the "off"-switch of their brain's neocortex. I have read stuff like "Making money", "Creating Jobs", "Bring peace and harmony to the world" and "Improve our local community". I'm serious!

There is no need to put "making money" there – after all, this form is a business registration, and operating at a profit (e.g. making money) is the most basic function of any business. No, you are not supposed to invent some type of altruistic or socialistic nonsense for this line item, in an attempt to cover up the fact that you are trying to earn a living.

What does belong in this space, however, is the result of the thought process which has hopefully matured to the point where you can tell what you intend to do within your business.

You plan to develop gaming software for computers? Then say so: "Gaming Software Development." It's not all that difficult, is it?

You would like to nurture your creative side and come up with gosh wonderful domain names for internet domains, register them in your name and then sell them for big bucks to interested buyers, which you first have to get interested? Then your business purpose will be "Trademark development and management" (a trademark or service mark is a name or picture, for example the aforementioned name of an internet domain).

Now that we've settled this question, we can move on to the less obvious part of your work: what exactly should your intended operation involve?

Cornerstones for selecting your business activity

Just in case no idea has surfaced what you could do for your business life: simply start with the basic reason why you wanted to or should start a business at all. That's most likely a quite decent point from which to start. Let's have a look at some common cases:

You are looking for ongoing ("residual") future income, derived from your work done today or tomorrow – and this income should continue to come in even if you can't or choose not to work at peak performance? Sickness, old age, accident – to name but a few.

In this case, you should exclude from the long list of potential activities all those, which do **not** feature the required benefit:

If you want income continuing even after you will be unable to perform physical labor, maybe you should cross "masseur" off your list.

In case you want to provide for a time of deteriorating mental ability to focus on your work at hand, you may want to discount the idea of going into business as a contract software developer.

Are you by chance a person who cannot handle psychical stress too well and can't or won't deal with aggressive, angry people – you may want to eliminate options like lawyer and accountant from your list.

It's fairly easy, but rarely done that way. Have you in the past accepted a job simply because you needed one, despite it not matching your skills and preferences? Looks like you know what I'm talking about.

You love talking and chatting with people? In this case, the sales person is allowed to stay on your list.

You enjoy talking on the phone? Maybe you should add wholesaler to the list, since nowadays lots of face-to-face contact actually takes place over the phone (and thus is not face-to-face, really). Yes, there are still in-person meetings on site, but only for larger sales volumes. For 500 Dollar sales, nobody in the wholesale segment drives anywhere to visit a customer.

Next cornerstone: How much money can you put into your business, and how much does it need?

That's a tricky one because startup owners reliably and always are underestimating the expenses of the startup, usually by a wide margin. The results of doing so are huge problems within a surprisingly short period, as I can attest from my daily environment:

I'm living on a Mediterranean island where there is a culture of self-employment, but no culture of entrepreneurship whatsoever. Most starting self-employed people are looking at their business as simply yet another job they got themselves (such point of view is widespread in most other countries, too. Rarely, though, have I seen it at the degree we experience here on the island).

Take it from somebody who has tried it for himself: this approach is dangerous and can easily end deadly, options of choice being a heart attack or a jump out of a skyscraper's uppermost floor.

Here on our island we have the situation of new restaurants going into business all the time – and closing down again about two weeks later because there was not enough revenue to pay the bills.

It's somewhat entertaining, since this way I can visit all types of different restaurants offering different cuisines, without actually having to go anywhere else. Russian, Italian, Lebanese, Moroccan – in short succession all at the same address. The operators of the respective restaurants are probably less than happy about it; if you are the startup owner experiencing something like that, you'll soon figure out why the aspect of available capital would have been an important one to consider.

As a matter of principle: make sure you can get over the first 6 months even with no money coming in at all. About how much money for those six months are we talking? Take this list as a starting point and ask yourself whether you would have thought of the items on it:

- Rent for the business premises (office, restaurant, whatever you need)
- Heating of the premises (or, in case you are starting in summer, you may need to consider cooling the premises); do you have to buy the heating/cooling devices?
- Security deposit for the rent (commonly worth 3 months of rent)
- Phone line or mobile phone contract (often both) plus connection fee
- Liability insurance (this one is mandatory)
- Legal costs insurance for the business (your private one will not cover the business affairs)
- Are you using your private car for the business? Take **twice** the government-set allowance for each mile you will be driving on behalf of your business (for example, that allowance rate would be US$ 0.535/mile for the US, or 0.45 Pound Sterling for the UK) – so, yes, you should calculate roughly 1$ or 1 Pound per mile as real costs
- Will you be using electric/electronic devices? Then calculate: the specified wattage, times number of hours running per day, times 30 days per month. This yields Wh. Divide that number by 1000 (to get to kWh) and multiply the result by your local price per kWh electricity; the result is the monthly cost for

electricity you need to come up with. In case you are not operating from home, you will need to add the base fee for you power connection – that can be anywhere up to 30 Dollar per month or so (business rate! That's not the cheap rate for residential power)

- Water consumption (even floors wish to be cleaned sometimes) and waste water disposal
- Does your local jurisdiction force you into some kind of mandatory membership? In that case, add their fees to your costs. This would include board memberships, as is common for many professionals like attorneys, doctors and the like. Look out for other such candidates – if in doubt, ask your local chamber of commerce. In Germany, for instance, you are by law a member of the chamber of commerce itself - alternatively the chamber of handicrafts - and neither is free
- Do you need to have employees or maintain business premises? Check with the laws and regulations regarding worker's comp; that frequently gets very expensive
- Do you need business internet or business email account? The costs for those should be added into your expenses
- Will you be hosting guests, whom you plan to offer coffee or other beverages? Make absolutely sure you know the respective health regulations inside out – and add the expenses for the beverages and any machines (espresso machine,…) to your costs
- Are you working with a company requiring an "entrance fee," for example a franchisor? Don't forget to include those, such fees are frequently remarkably high (take the golden arches, for example. Their entrance fee easily amounts to several hundred thousand up into the millions, depending on location). On top of that, such companies commonly demand monthly fees plus advertising cost sharing (which is not optional), quickly exploding any budget unless it's planned very diligently
- Will you be operating a retail location? If so, there are no ifs and buts, you will need shop fittings and furnishings, initial product stock and the like; we will get to that topic in a bit, just be patient
- Business registration; most municipalities (cities, counties) require you to main a registration for your business. You should

not be too surprise if that business registration or business license comes with a price tag – ask your city about it. In any case, you should expect between 20 Euros (as found in Continental Europe) up to several hundred Dollars (in many US states) for the mere privilege of doing business.

- Incorporation or organization costs – if you want to incorporate your business (e.g. form a legal entity with limited liability, so you are somewhat shielded against business risks), ask your secretary of state or the local court about the costs for doing so. The fees involved are substantial...

- Costs for a certified public accountant or at least a tax preparer, who will deal with the revenue department on your behalf. No matter how little business volume you expect to generate in the first year – you will need an accountant. Unless you are looking for the fastest path to paranoia - in which case simply go ahead without an accountant on your side of the table. Consider this: the robber barons of revenue castle don't even speak your language. I have some doubts you are too eager to learn yet another seriously foreign language (assuming the language of business, too, is still foreign to you); so, for any chance of survival you need somebody who speaks your language **and** theirs. Such guys are called public accountants, and they want to get paid. So – add in their cost for the first year, which will easily approach 1000 Dollar/Pound/Euro even for a minor business

- Any additional machines or pieces of equipment you will definitely need? Look up their prices and add them to your costs. Think of things like PC, laptop, phones etc.

Obviously, this list is still incomplete. Let's hope I was able to direct you to the right train of thought, so you can come up with all the stuff that you and I didn't think of, so far.

Now it's time to live up to my promise and move on to your initial inventory and first stock for retail businesses. I have experienced over and again how business startups (including my own) believed to get by without buying initial inventory. Just wait for the orders coming in and buy the goods when needed, what's the problem? By that time, you have the money from your customer, so you can afford to buy the merchandise.

Well, there are problems with this approach. Big ones, which will render this obvious way of doing business useless and risky.

Here is one reason: the internet is pretty much ubiquitous and every potential customer knows he or she can find the products cheaper online than if they would buy from you, at least if they look long and hard.

Then why would anybody buy from your local store or even from your internet web site, rather than from some cheaper supplier online? For one reason, and one reason only: because the goods are available right away and the customer can take stuff home immediately. That's by far the most important individual reason! (Yeah, there it is again, instant gratification)

Oh – the customer can't take the merchandise home right away because you didn't carry inventory? Too bad, in this case she will thank you for the nice and comprehensive advice, leave your store and order the item somewhere online for half price. As easy as that. It should be inherently obvious that you will not be able to make any profit from this type of business conduct. Please, don't even try to convince yourself otherwise. Enough people have tried before you. The outcome didn't change.

But, so you say, you are doing business on the internet yourself? People are ordering online, so they don't know you don't have any products in stock?

Turns out, that is a problem by itself. If you do not own the inventory but nevertheless are already collecting the customer's payment (which commonly happens automatically if you use one of the usual payment processing services), then you are walking on very thin legal ice. In many jurisdictions, you have just committed a crime by accepting the money without actually owning the product. You believe you are not affected by such odd jurisdictions? Well, as we know, the web is worldwide – how can you make sure your customer doesn't happen to be resident of just such a jurisdiction? Do you really think your online store can live without any customers from the USA or France, Japan or some other "odd" jurisdiction?

Let's assume you can settle this legal delicacy somehow. Leaves you with the initial problem already encountered in our brick & mortar store situation:

If you receive the customer order and only then are going to purchase the goods yourself, how much of an "instant gratification" event does that provide for your customer? Not much of, I'd say. Do you expect your customers to wait 2 or 3 weeks for their purchase to arrive in the mail? Forget it, those times are long gone. Today, if you can't provide tracking details of the parcel service to your customer within hours after the customer clicked the "Buy now" button on your web site, you can safely consider the order cancelled. The customer can always return the merchandise to you or – even more likely – simple refuse to accept the package, should it finally arrive at some time. Or even worse: accept the package and cancel the credit card charge anyway.

Why would customers do something evil like that? Because you failed to deliver on time, that's why. And believe me, it doesn't matter what you write in your fine print aka terms of service: for the customer, only the customer's expectation counts. Get used to it.

Returning to the brick & mortar store example – how much merchandise, would you say, you need for a very small store, even a tiny one? I'd say, at least enough to make the shelves appear well-stocked. Don't mind the fact that your "inventory warehouse" consists only of those shelves – that indeed the customer would not know. The shelves, however, are in plain sight. And that's where the customer will go to have a look, grab the package, turn it and feel it as if that would give him or her a realistic impression of the product's quality. And, that's where the customer takes the stuff from before he pays you. So you better fill the shelves!

How much merchandise you will need, that should depend a good deal on what it is that you are selling and how many shelves your store is housing.

How is your small store going to look like? Will you have a counter, which is home to the cash register (the latter hopefully included in the list of expenses as a machine you had to pay for, the former in the list of furniture – also an expense)? Behind the counter, there will be standing you, and behind you a minimum of 3 shelves (basic business rules – never less than 3).

Additionally and psychologically absolutely required, there has to be another shelf on the side of the store room – that provides visitors with an opportunity to look at something else than you. If you are standing behind your counter, the customer will have to look "at" you even when gazing at the shelves behind you. If you don't provide an opportunity for the customer's gaze to wander someplace else, you will see people exiting your store faster than you can say "Hello."

Grab a measurement tape and check out the width of the shelves you plan to use. How wide are they? Maybe 60"? Good, let's go with those 60" and work with that number. How many floor layers are inside your shelf rack? 5, in your case? Good, let me sum it up so far:

4 shelf racks (3 behind the counter, one on the side for not having to stare at you) with 5 floors each, for a total of 20 floors. Each one being 60" – that's a total of 1200 inch, i.e. 100 ft space which wants to be filled with products.

How large is the package of your products? Obviously, at this point in the book, I have not even a clue what you will be selling or how large that package may be – so I am going to make up some numbers out of thin air.

Let's assume you are going to sell Nevada Green Algae food supplements (not that those exist – but I did say I am pulling them from thin air, right?). Such capsules usually come in plastic bottles sticking in standardized cardboard boxes 2.6" wide, 2.6" deep, and 3" tall.

The 3 inch height turn out to be an issue because the shelf floors have easily 13" space between them – that means, the customer can immediately see with his own eyes how many boxes are tucked behind each other in your shelves.

Therefore, you will have to place a minimum of 3 boxes in a row to give the impression of at least a decent inventory – which would make sense anyway because, after all, the products on the shelves **are** your inventory and are needed to make money by being sold, right?

At 2.6" box width, we can get away with using 3" per row in the shelf – that means, 20 rows per shelf floor, for a total of 400 rows (=20 rows per shelf x 20 shelve floors). Each row being 3 boxes deep, you will need 1200 product boxes to make your shelves appear well stocked, at a minimum. Those 1200 boxes you will need to buy upfront, before even welcoming your first potential customer into your store.

How much will those Nevada Green Algae cost you at wholesale price? Let's assume 20 Dollar each box, so we are looking at 1200 x 20 = 24000 Dollar without any stretch of the imagination. Let me spell it out: Twenty-Four Thousand Dollar. That's just for the first shipment.

If you can sell the goods at a price of 30 per bottle, then you have to immediately plug 20 of that money back into re-ordering the product – after all, you don't want to run out of stock. Therefore, don't assume for a single moment those 30 would be available in full do anything else with it.

How long does it take from ordering your products until they arrive at your door step? Right next day? Great, in this case you may continue to calculate using those the numbers as we figured them out so far.

The delay between ordering and receiving shipment is more like 3 weeks? Then you have a slightly larger problem at hand. That means you have to know 3 weeks **upfront** how much product you will be selling over those 3 next weeks. Which, of course, is not called "knowing," the more honest term would be "guessing." Let's make it at least an educated guess:

If your plan calls for the sales of 50 product items per day, then you ought to be selling 900 of your bottles within a 3-week period. Oh… since you had only 1200 bottles, selling 900 of those will leave your shelves rather empty, worsening progressively as time goes on and stuff is sold. It won't be long before your little store conjures up associations with the times of communism, when the store shelves were essentially empty. Right now, people in Venezuela are experiencing just that, and they are not exactly happy about it – your customers won't be happy, either. Consequently, they most likely won't be your customers for much longer. So, if you plan for selling 900 bottles in 3 weeks **and** the lead time between order and shipment arrival averages 3 weeks, we should re-work your reorder strategy a bit:

If you order the second shipment right on the day your store opens its doors for the first time, you can expect the new delivery 3 weeks later; at that time, your stock will have depleted down to about 300 bottles

– ok, you say, you think that's something you could work with, but the fresh supply really shouldn't come later than that. Nevada Green Algae will be a product in huge demand, after all – according to your business idea. Therefore, you simply go ahead and order the second 900 bottles on the eve of your store's grand opening.

When doing so, an almost negligible little problem is crossing your path: since you are still startup business, vendors like the Nevada Green Algae's manufacturer won't make trade credit available to you, i.e. you have to pay upfront. From their point of view, quite reasonable, you still have no clue when you will get the money from your own sales – so they better make sure they get their money right away. For you, that means you have the questionable privilege of forking out those 900 x 20 = 18000 dollars additionally, bringing your total cost of goods up to 42000, with all of those costs demanding to get paid before you sell your first bottle.

Why is that a problem? Well... do you actually **have** those 42000 Dollar right from the get-go?

You do? Oh great, I am relieved. Then let us quickly proceed to sell – you will need all the revenue you can get!

Assuming you can sell each of the 1200 bottles in their neat cardboard boxes for the 30 Dollar you were aiming at, then your gross profit share of that amount is only somewhere between 8 and 10; the rest goes to the manufacturer because you had to buy the bottles, to the department of revenue if you are selling in an area where you are burdened with VAT or where the sales tax comes out of the quoted price (Canada and Europe, for example) rather than being tacked on top of it (as is common in the US).

For the sake of calculation, let's go with the $8 – better safe than sorry. In this case, selling 1200 bottles per month generate a gross profit of slightly more than 10K (10K = 10000). You're set, that's wonderful, isn't it?

Indeed, it's a remarkable result. That's why you need to have a careful look at the numbers. Something starts coming up in the back of your mind... oh, right - there are ongoing expenses to be paid. Those nasty little critters on the list of recurring expenses (you do remember those, right?) like (especially) rent, electricity, water, and their likes.

After you paid those annoyances, your profits have diminished a bit towards roughly 9000 – still not bad. Up to the point of answering the question how you are going to pay for your livelihood. And that of your family, if you have one and need to pay for it, too.

No problem, you say – that can be easily done with only 3000. Well then – leaves you with 6000 in the business. Still a great buffer for times to come, right?

Erm… if you plan to take 3000 out of the business for family purposes, then consequently you need to also take the taxes for that money out of the business. If you are in your store all day, you will need to pay for your own health insurance one way or the other. How specifically this is calculated, depends greatly on the country you are living in; if you are living in an area where you simply can buy health insurance on your own, you frequently got the better end of the stick – provided that you actually DO purchase insurance. Should you happen to live in a country with a socialized insurance scheme (Canada, Europe) then you pay for it with higher taxes or some percentage of your income. Those percentages are frequently a problem for sole proprietors (not so much if you incorporated your business) because you have to pay a percentage of your taxable income, not a percentage of the amount you take out of the business. In our example, that means: you are paying social insurance contributions based on the 9000, not on the 3000 you actually withdrew.

The problem with the "taxable income" versus the actual amount withdrawn also materializes for purposes of retirement contributions (such as Social Security in the US, where the according tax for self-employeds is called "Self-Employment Tax"). Typical amounts eaten by the governments under the presumption of saving for your retirement pensions (which they don't do, by the way) run in the neighborhood of 15% (USA) and 20% (Germany). The United Kingdom is the outlier here: The British rules combine social security and health care into one percentage amount, which runs between 6% and 9% for most part.

For the sake of ease, let's assume you will end up with 1500 for income taxes and 600 for your health insurance (clearly, that assumes you are the only person to be covered; additional covered family members add to the costs).

That leaves you with maybe 3900 per month as profits.

Now the big blue elephant in the room – how do you manage to sell 50 bottles per day? To who?

When, in a former life, I was working for a larger computer retailer in the middle of the shopping district of a major affluent city in Central Europe, we did experience individual days when the entire revenue consisted of a single sale of 2 or 3 printer cartridges. Those days were 99.7% below the revenue we needed to just cover the costs of this branch for that day. That should give you an idea how rough things can get.

I myself made the mistake of coming to believe these incidents to "only happen to that company" due to some unknown mistake they made. Consequently, I didn't plan for such days when I ventured into my own business later – which did ok until Iraq War I happened. In the moment this war started, sales collapsed to Zero. Not just "very low" or "painfully low" but literally zero. Nada. Nothing.

It stayed that way not just for a day or two. It went on for weeks. Actually, nothing went on. The economy was plain dead. When it recovered, it was too late for us – my company was toast. Now, is my bankruptcy back then the fault of George H.W. Bush, who forced the troops into Iraq? Nope. It was my fault. I was the one who didn't plan for it. As a result, I was the one who didn't prepare the business to take advantage of a situation like this. How could anyone take advantage of something like this? Well, companies like mine were unprepared and sold their goods at whatever prices, as long as the buyers paid immediately, preferably in cash. Forget about recovering the costs – everybody needed hard cash to pay the bills and to live on. If your company was prepared, you could go out on a shopping spree at fire sale prices. If you are unprepared, you are the one selling at those very fire sale prices.

So – you had better prepare for slow days, maybe even some more than just a few. There will be days when you don't sell the expected 50 bottles. Probably not even 5. On top of that, you will have to actively market your products and your store – which should turn out difficult if you are occupied in the store all day.

How do you fix this issue now? Well, usually you have two options: either you hire some part-time employee, or you do everything yourself and extend your working hours into late night.

As I see it, you really can't afford any of those two options. Here's why:

It won't take too many night shifts before the rest of the world can visually experience what you are going through. Nobody wants to speak to a sales person with pale skin, dark rings around the eyes, and who is yawning after every 6th word. Not to mention how convincing your sales pitch for a presumably healthy food supplement may turn out to be. Do I really want to swallow those odd Nevada Green Algae pills, if **that** is the result?

If you decide to hire a helping hand who is willing to work sufficiently long and productive in your store, then you quickly will figure out that you can't get it much cheaper than 2000 Dollar (including government overhead).

Now, let's play through a month with so few slow days that, in effect, you are losing only about 5 days of revenue (if you lose so few days, consider yourself lucky!). That means you will have a good 2100 Dollar less gross profit than previously planned, but now with 2000 Dollar higher costs. So, you are now looking at a difference of 4100 Dollar. That's the "uh-oh" moment: previously, you were looking at 3900 profit, now reduce that by 4100 – and you have to face the fact that you are now operating at a cash loss!

Without pestering you with the details any more – I hope I did manage to show how easy it is to end up in loss territory. Which is not good.

When you are under stress and your business is running at a loss, I fear for your ability to convincingly present to your potential customers why they should pay 30 Dollar per bottle in your store instead of buying them for 17 Dollar somewhere from a mail-order company. (Yeah, it's true – as soon as you have paid for your orders, your customers will find sources selling the products for less than your own purchase price. The universe may not conspire against you, but it certainly doesn't go out of its way to be of any help)

But let's be kind to our freshly baked startup business owner (that would be you). Assume for now that you are actually able to work day shift plus night shift and still won't appear like a zombie. In this case, your business might end up with maybe 900 per month.

Oh – well, you not only wanted to plan marketing campaigns, you also wanted to execute on them, right? Woosh... there the money goes.

No, it's not a joke. Precisely that's how everyday business looks for many business startups. After a brief love affair with the "self-employment" sweetheart, a steep fall back down to earth leads to a painful encounter with something called reality. Quite commonly, a brick & mortar retail store doesn't produce just no income for the first 12 months, but instead frequently generates cash losses and further need for capital.

A note on the side: I am emphasizing the "cash loss" because there are indeed other types of losses, which are non-cash in nature. Those are as dangerous in the end, but they don't kill you over the course of just a few months. Cash losses, however, will do just that.

If we sum it up so far: you did start with 42000 just for the initial two orders for product stock. Now it appears that – even if your business doesn't fold right away – you won't see any of these 42K back in your pocket over at least the next year. That, by the way, is the exact reason why bankers are more than just hesitant to lend this money to you – bankers know statistics, too.

Since you are not seeing any part of the 42K back during that time, how would you be able to service the bank loan – which includes not only repayment installments but also interests on top of that? The answer may be easy, but it's certainly not pleasant: you cannot. More precisely, if you have to borrow the money for startup costs, your business is most likely technically broke before you opened the front door for the very first time.

Have I convinced you to let go of the idea for a retail business? In this case, I wish to beg for forgiveness – it was not actually my intention to do so.

What I wanted to make perfectly clear: your chances of economic survival in a retail business are slim to none, if you didn't plan ahead very diligently.

Why does nobody call this type of self-employment a fraud, a scam, or a plain rip-off?

Because nobody said it would be easy. It's important you keep in mind how difficult starting a business in retail will be — anywhere on the planet, and pretty much regardless of what you are selling.

Despite all that, retail can be seriously great idea. Maybe, just maybe, we have to make some changes in our perception of how retail should work. Stop asking for reality to adjust to our expectations and instead adjust our plans to reality. Sounds like a concept?

Retail today

Contrary to popular belief, the retail companies have to fulfill a function today probably more important than ever before: bringing together demand and supply. Which is pretty much what any market is supposed to do, anyway.

However, today we are looking at a worldwide supply of an immense product spectrum and also a worldwide demand for many products. Thanks to this situation, the real service in demand is not the production of even more goods. Instead, the one commodity in high demand is the ability to match demand and supply in a way that yields the most benefits for both sides involved. Since the early 1800s, thanks to David Ricardo, we know that this matching job unlocks value for everybody — even for an inefficient producer. However, we have made surprisingly little progress when it comes to explaining this most important aspect of all markets to our customers, our governments, and our manufacturers.

As a result, we can source our cooking spoons worldwide — but hardly anybody in our neighborhood would know where you could actually obtain the cooking spoon with the best value for money. That's partially due to "value" being a quite personal aspect, hence different for every individual. The other — bigger — part is that we are exposed to a huge flood of "buy now" advertising all around us. In other terms: we are suffering information overload. If you want to call TV commercials "information."

That said, we saw the resulting problems in the previous sections of this book: the business model of a traditional retailer is deeply flawed. The obvious problem is the huge strain on your capital with, at the same time, very low profit margins (margins are the price differentials between the wholesale price and the retail price).

Oh, and something else is quite faulty: the belief, everybody could simply go ahead and open a store with little in terms of pre-requirements. As we have seen, that's not true today. A brief glance at history reveals: it also hasn't been true in the past. There is a reason merchants frequently were well situated even before they opened up shop. That's because they had to be. For that reason, history has provided us with literal dynasties of merchant families and international traders – who else would have the required personal relationships to product sources, sufficient credibility and renown with buyers and, on top of that, sufficient capital to bear the risks involved?

Fortunately, times have changed – provided the entrepreneur is willing to change his thinking models as well. We can learn a great deal from a company called "Teekampagne," (translates to Tea Campaign) established and operated by Professor Günter Faltin from Germany's university FU Berlin. He has capably – and impressively – demonstrated how to set up a new company and break into established markets by simply changed one's own thought patterns.

Facts: tea retail

Before we can appreciate (and benefit from) how Faltin improved the tea retail trade business model, we had better first understand what it is that he improved upon.

Tea is being routed to Europe and America via quite ancient pathways. Coming from the tea plantations in India and China, it travels through importers to the international tea exchange in London, several national importers and repackers (who like to call themselves 'brand name manufacturers'), wholesalers and retailers – and I did omit easily half of the intermittent stops.

We consumers now have the option to purchase the tea from a tea boutique store (at high cost and hopefully matching quality) or from a regular supermarket (usually slightly less high priced and at a presumably slightly lower quality).

Let's have a look at how much processing the product 'tea' has experienced along its travel from the plantation's front gate to the store shelf. Fairly easy to figure out: not at all. The tea has been repacked just once, but other than that nothing changed. Specifically, no product improvement was necessary. The tea on the shelf is pretty much the same product as it was at the time it left the plantation.

How then is it possible our store prices frequently amount to more than 10x the price paid to the plantation company in India?

The high store prices are not just a result from a very long and tedious chain of importers and wholesalers. The other problem is: there are literally hundreds of different types of black tea (not to mention green tea or white tea), all of which we expect our merchant to have stocked for us. After all, they all have different price tags, and no customer wants to be left behind – so the merchant will have to offer several layers of price and quality of black tea.

By providing what the customers demand, the merchants run into exactly the same trap you have seen in your hypothetical small store with the Nevada Green Algae: the required capital to fund the product inventory turns out to be gargantuan, especially when compared to the profit the retailer can derive from those small packages of tea (and therefore from this tremendously expensive inventory).

Weapon of choice: self-restraints

Professor Faltin, not a tea drinker himself, has asked a very simple question: if there are so many different types of tea offered only due to the different price point – shouldn't there be one type of tea pretty much everybody considers "the best"?

Tea lovers surely know the answer: of course there is. It's a tea from the district Darjeeling in India's Himalayas. However, right away comes the catch, this tea also happens to be much too expensive for most people's everyday consumption. Which is why those most people fall back on cheaper alternatives like tea from Ceylon or Assam.

Faltin's next thought then was the proverbial blinding flash of the obvious: what if we would offer nothing but this one "best of all teas"? By doing so, the company would not need to stock more than exactly this one type of tea. Consequently, no capital cost for other inventory. That alone would lower the costs for the remaining one type of tea substantially. This, in turn, could be used to lower the retail price for this tea. Then, so Faltin's logic, the company should be able to sell much more of the high-quality tea at then-lower prices, which in turn enables him to buy in larger volumes and obtain far better prices, maybe even to cut out the middle men – if you buy large quantities, that ought to be possible. Which in turn allows reducing the retail price even further. And so on.

I guess it is unnecessary to point out how little Faltin has been taken serious – by anybody. The large corporate competition neither wanted him in the business nor considered him anything but a lunatic, and the middle men (which he wanted to cut out) could have hardly been less pleased.

But it is worthwhile remarking that Faltin's Tee-Kampagne today happens to be the largest exporter of Darjeeling tea from India (and since there is no other Darjeeling region, that makes Faltin the largest exporter of Darjeeling tea worldwide). And - he is the largest by a wide margin.

That's all nice, you say – but this market niche now is occupied. So why do I tell you about it?

I'm so glad you asked.

The genius of Faltin's company is not the product, since he obviously didn't invent nor improve the black tea.

By merely re-evaluating the way things were done in this line of business, he was able to make substantial changes to the cost structure – to the point that nowadays he can offer the best tea at prices previously considered low even for mediocre sorts. **That** was his door opener into this market.

The other part of his brilliance becomes clear when you ask for the number of hours Faltin has to spend on running that business. What do you think is possible? 12 hours daily? (Most self-employed people work about 16 hours per day!) Maybe only 8? Or might it be possible this genius needs only... 4?

Did you just consider the "only 4 hours" even an option? Quite a daring thought, right? Well, the 4 hours are not all that far-fetched. He needs more like 2 to 4 hours a day – **once a week**!

Yeah, you might be shrugging your shoulders; it's nice to have enough money to be able to afford all those employees taking care of business. Might be so, but that would be missing the point. The everyday work in Faltin's business is **not** performed by employees – at least not his employees.

Günter Faltin has built his entire company from service modules offered by **other** companies!

Accounting? That's what accountants are for.

Customer service? There's a whole call center industry offering this service on the cheap for anybody wanting to use it.

Shipping, transport, and customs handling upon arrival in the country of destination? For those tasks, somebody long ago had invented logistics service providers, who specialize in doing just these tasks. All you have to do is issue the order, wait for the invoice, pay it, and you're set.

How does Faltin get the huge wooden boxes containing the tea from the shipping container to his front door and, even more critical, into his home?

Simple – he doesn't. The logistics company is shipping the wooden boxes and containers directly to a fulfillment service provider, who repackages the tea from the huge wooden boxes into retail-friendly package sizes and then sends those as small parcels to the customers. Which customers? Of course to the customers whose address and order information has been provided to this company by Faltin's Tee-Kampagne.

Yeah, you read that right: this man never sees the product he is selling.

How does he get his money? That's what specialized service companies are for, commonly called banks or financial service providers.

Marketing, advertising, press releases – there are ample highly specialized people in highly specialized companies available for Faltin, for you or for anybody else willing to pay them. Those specialists over time have become seriously good at what they are doing. Why would Faltin want to replicate all their learning process to finally arrive at a fraction of their expertise, making a do-it-yourself approach far more expensive than just buying those services? Of course he wouldn't – and nor should you.

What can you glean from Faltin? At least that much: business owners need not and should not re-invent the wheel over and over again. If there is already a solution for a problem, usually you can pay somebody to get the job done at low cost. This we should keep in mind for the rest of this book.

How would I know how things are done?

So, there's a great idea in your head (or so you think) and you even have managed to save up some money, which should be sufficient to get the business idea off the ground – but unfortunately you have no remote clue how this industry is operating?

Maybe you plan to set up a Chinese Restaurant in your home town?

I hope you have planned for a sizeable chunk of cash to pay for the goldfish tank cleaning. Don't need to because your vision doesn't include a goldfish tank? In this case, you may want to consider investing in learning about the art of Chinese restaurant management, first.

Chinese Restaurants are chronically threatened by the Chinese counterpart of the better-known Italian Mafia. However, unlike their Italian equivalents, the Chinese Mafiosi at least hand you a receipt for the extorted money – to make sure the IRS, HMRC and their likes aren't knocking at their door steps, being tipped off by large amounts disappearing from the official accounts of the victim's business. What would those invoices claim that the payment was for?

Surely nobody wants to write "extortion" or "protection contribution" on the invoice, right? Nope, according to those invoices, the billed service is "fish tank specialist cleaning" or something similar.

Seriously, you didn't know that until now? Oh well. But you probably didn't want to do the Chinese restaurant thing anyway, did you?

Of course not – you were more looking into a bar or pub style thing. No Chinese Mafia there. And you probably are aware of the ins and outs of lease negotiations for your location, right? The usual things like trading a substantially reduced rent over the initial years for exclusive distribution of one brewery's beer, and stuff... Why would a brewery go for that? Because they happen to frequently be the owner of the place you are renting, that's why.

All this restaurant stuff is not your cup of tea? Ok, how about the proverbial candy store? After all, summer is about done and you would like to make your profit mainly in the Christmas season. Wouldn't that be the perfect time to go about it?

Great idea, let's get going – speaking of it, you did place your product orders back in March, didn't you? No? Oh, that's too bad – the manufacturers are producing for "the season" only what has been ordered at the beginning of the year. Whatever you haven't ordered earlier this year, you will not receive before the year is over. Too bad. Did that catch you unprepared? Hm...

Every industry, every line of business has its own unwritten rules. You had better know those rules before you start; otherwise you are out of business quicker than you have gotten into it.

Which brings us to the 2 main road blocks in your path to success:

1. Do you know your way around in your line of business? Which are the legal restrictions and which de-facto rules are there?
2. How much experience do you have when it comes to selling – selling yourself as a credible person, as well as selling products or services?

Please note – the questions are "**Do** you **know**" and "**do** you **have**."

Not "Can you see yourself figuring out how..." and "Could you maybe vaguely recall..."

What I'm trying to say is this: once you have poured you life's savings and 120% of your physical and mental energy into your startup, it may well be far too late to learn the tricks and gimmicks of this line of business. Can you afford to lose all that cash and end up being burnt out? Unlikely to happen to you? Keep in mind: a major share of self-employed people has been bankrupt at least once in their life (at least factually bankrupt, the formal act of filing for bankruptcy is for most part irrelevant).

Let me say this: it's absolutely true; entrepreneurship and business ownership are our best chances for a fulfilled and happy life I know. However, those two are also the fastest roads to financial hell and deep depression.

How can you as a newbie or layperson set the switches to avoid this hell and depression thing, and instead end up with the happy and fulfilled life?

You won't believe how simple it is: learn it.

Well, it takes a second glance to notice something less obvious. Learn from who? Study at some kind of university and take courses in entrepreneurship or business administration? In that case, be aware you are trying to learn from somebody who himself most likely never has been a business owner. Instead, you will receive advice from career academics or bureaucrats about how they imagine business should work. Essentially, you are buying fictional entertainment unrelated to reality. At least to your reality.

Ok, try to think about the problem again. Learn from who? Right — you need somebody who knows his way around where you want to go. Some kind of helper for your startup. Preferably someone who has a vested interested in you being successful.

Kickstart

Basically, there are 4 different types of persons helping you with your business startup — let's run them through, so you get to know your options.

Of course, you can try it without one. After all, you have your pride, right? True, and briefly thereafter you will have the questionable honor of being member of the statistical group of businesses collapsing within 5 years after starting. And this is a huge group. Depending on the statistics you are looking at, those failures run between 60% and 95% of startups (regardless of the exact number: it's the majority). Of 100 new startups, up to 95 will fail — that's a painful picture.

The Mentor

Probably the best approach is finding somebody who has already accomplished what you want to do. Somebody who is already where you want to be.

Should you find someone like that, who on top of his qualifications also happens to be willing to mentor you — consider yourself lucky and do whatever he demands for tutoring you.

The Partner

Another option is to seek out somebody who has all the skills and knowledge you are lacking – and then invite that person to become joint owner in your business. The basic idea is the same as in a mentoring situation, and in theory it should work all the same. In reality, however, a co-owner will never be able to review your ideas as unprejudiced as somebody who is not at risk of losing his livelihood due to your decisions in the business. After all, a joint partner stands to lose wealth and reputation if you screw up – then, how can you expect that partner to look out for you rather than for himself first?

Once you have invited a partner in the house, you won't get rid of him that easily. For a good reason: he is more or less as much owner of the business as you are. It's not just your own company anymore, it's now the company owned by your partner and you together.

If both of you have similar powers and responsibilities for the overall structure, then you can safely assume that nobody will feel responsible. Even if you cannot imagine today doing that in the future, you will very likely start dumping the unpleasant stuff on your partner. That person, in turn, either will do the same to you, or will eventually collapse under the burden you dropped on him. Both versions are not beneficial to anybody. Instead, a joint ownership/partnership is commonly a surefire path to catastrophe, mutual finger pointing and financial ruin. Yes, there are exceptions. Alas, just as the term implies: they are exceptions, not the norm.

The Franchisor

The entire concept of franchising got on its way essentially after WWII. Basically, it's the idea of one business owner developing the business model and standardizing all intrinsic details of its operations. The standardization and detailed description of every step along the way makes it possible to only need a brief and simple training of new workers to result in predictable results of (hopefully) high quality. It's the idea of not hiring superb people, but average people doing things in a superb way.

This concept, usually including the related product shipments, is rented by other business owners, called franchisees. The franchisees essentially pay for the work they didn't want to do – namely develop the entire business model, train their staff and market the brand name. Since those aspects are among the most valuable parts of a business, franchisors frequently charge dearly for them. In system gastronomy (e.g. burger fast food chains), we are speaking of several hundreds of thousand dollars just as the initial entry fee; but it won't end with the entry – there will be advertising fees, ongoing monthly base fees, ongoing monthly revenue share and so on.

To judge from their success, many of those franchise systems are well worth their cost – the only problem being their enormous capital requirements and consequently their risk.

Network-Marketing / MLM

Network marketing combines elements of the other three approaches, which yields a unique structure – and which requires diligence before getting in on it.

Network marketing organizations are very different in some aspects, simply because there are so many of them. Nevertheless, some aspects they all have in common, at least conceptually:

You have at least one mentor, commonly several of them – your immediate mentor, your mentor's mentor and so on. Your immediate mentor has just slightly more experience than you do, which is why this mentor has such a great understanding and empathy for your issues and questions – he himself just went through the same.

The more complex and specific your questions are becoming over time, the higher in the list of your mentors you will have to go before you find someone with the correct answer for you. This way, network marketing circumvents the problem of requiring one individual mentor to have all answers for everything. Instead, it's more like "average people having great answers, **collectively.**"

Mostly, all of your mentors at the same time are participating to some degree in your success – but they do not own any part of your business. Whenever you buy products (or services) from the network company, your mentors get a small share of that revenue. However, you do not have to pay this mentoring fee on top of the purchase price – instead, it's already baked into the fixed prices charged for the products.

Similar to franchising models, network companies are usually providing you with guidance, manuals, and online education aimed at helping you build and grow your own business.

Normally, the fundamental concept is very easy to grasp because you as a business starter are not supposed to occupy yourself with prerequisites and long planning cycles. Network companies for all intents and purposes are "Sign & Go" types of business models, permitting quick start within a few days and quick early successes – essential to preventing the new business owner's spiral into depression (which all too often happens when you go into business all by yourself).

While franchisees are required to go through extensive training provided (for a fee) by the franchisor (even if that part is too often skipped for cost reasons), network marketing is based on the assumption that you will have no employees at all. Your business is designed as essentially a one-man-show, and the self-perpetuating effect later will be achieved not by means of hiring employees. Instead, you will save yourself the employee headaches and invite other budding business starters into you network – at which time you will become their mentor and will be compensated for mentoring (and having mentored) them.

Precisely this concept of network marketing is what the rest of the book revolves around. No other business model is as badly understood, no other model is frequently explained as lousy, and hardly any other model is abused so often as vehicle for outright fraud.

Those 3 facts of life fully justify to have a closer look at network marketing; there really is no need to fall prey to fraudsters or lose or shirt due to ignorant people who lead us into illegal or damaging "opportunities", regardless of how well-meaning those suggestions might have been (or not).

What does network marketing do?

As we should somewhat expect from businesses bearing the term "marketing" in their name, the focus of network marketing obviously would be marketing, i.e. the attempt to sell something to somebody. That's good to know – now we only need to figure out what supposedly is being sold to whom.

Let me pick up some pieces of information we have left in our tea retail store, which – easily identifiable – is selling tea. Such a store would obtain the goods to be sold from a wholesaler or an importer, sometimes directly from the London Tea Exchange – and is affording huge sums of money to do so.

In case of the tea trade, it is fairly obvious how the merchant is attempting to make a profit (which is what a business needs to pay the owner), namely the retailer is buying at one price (called wholesale price) and selling at a higher price (called retail price). The difference between them is the reason for bothering to move the boxes around the world.

As a surprise to some, this is not the only possible source of profits for a retailer. Quite a while ago, large supermarket chains have noticed the nasty fact that they can't make a living from buying and selling stuff; they have run into the very same problem we have discovered when we tried to calculate the capital needed for your Nevada Green Algae supplements: the demand for capital is gigantic, the tied-up capital continues to cost further money, you need expensive employees and ultimately you risk being stuck with unsellable products; that's especially true if you are dealing with products having a short shelf life, such as most food items.

In a stroke of genius, large-scale retailers decided to let their shelf space instead of stocking those shelves themselves. Somebody else is renting that shelf space in the store on a per-shelf-floor base and paying the retailer rent for the privilege of being allowed to put products up for sale. Who would be willing to pay rent for that privilege? The manufacturer of the items, of course.

In essence, the retail store's customers are not buying from the retail store in many cases but instead directly from the manufacturer. This manufacturer has to pay rent for the shelf, plus a sales-dependent commission on top of that. Under this arrangement, the supermarket neither has to fork out the money to stock products, nor is it the supermarket's problem if products end up spoiled or unsaleable. The function of the retail store is reduced to collecting money from the customer and making sure customers show up in the store, to begin with.

However, despite this shift of risk from the retailer to the manufacturer, we still can easily identify where the retailer's revenue stream is coming from: selling products, of course. Even if the manufacturer is technically the one paying the retailer for the shelf space, all payments directly or indirectly come from the retailer offering and selling products to paying customers. Without customers purchasing something, there will be no payments to the store and no payments to the manufacturer.

Regardless whether you are looking at a supermarket operating under a rent-the-shelf method or you are examining a small-shop tea retailer buying and selling his own inventory: any profits, actually any revenue, comes from selling something to an end-customer. In some cases, that "something" might be a service instead of a product – some 3rd party company provides a service, and the retailer sells that service and outsources the actual work. In these cases, the retailer is trading that service just as if it would have been a product – which is why "product" usually refers to products as well as services.

Those previous sections provide us with an important insight – as obvious as it may sound right now, keep it in mind for dealing with anything you are offered under the catch-all phrase "network marketing" or "MLM." What we have been able to, quite easily, identify has been the intended source of income for the retailer.

When you are faced with a business proposal, you should able to see where your profit is supposed to come from, immediately and without delicate understanding of complex presentations. Is it derived from the sales of goods or services, preferably at prices common for that type of product in the markets? If so – good, you may continue evaluating this opportunity.

You have a hard time figuring out from which end-customer activity your income is proposed to originate? Ask. And ask again, and do so openly and clearly: where is the profit coming from, economically speaking? If even after a clear question, you still are not offered a clear and easy response, then the most likely answer is that there is no profit to be had. Neither now nor in the future. At least not for you.

The problem with the source of profits

Why is this question of the profit source so important? Isn't the ultimate source irrelevant, as long as you're being paid at all?

Unfortunately no. There are two aspects you need to keep in mind whenever you are trying to decide upon network marketing concepts. Those are the same for all other types of business as well, but nowhere else can they be hidden that easily. Namely:

1. If your profits are sourced from illegal sources, you won't be too happy with them. The victims of illegal activities as well as the government will get back to you and retrieve all that presumed profit from you – and then some, as compensation for damages and as penalties. That's true even if you didn't notice the whole thing being illegal. You have conspired with the ones who knew it to be illegal, and as such you are a collaborator with a criminal – which makes you a criminal, too. This is a huge risk, and right now it's prevalent all over the marketplace under the disguise of so-called "Bitcoin networks." We'll get into those a bit more on coming pages

2. If you assume you don't see the source of profits because there aren't any, but instead the scheme is laid out so you and your buddies are simply ripping off unsuspecting fools – then keep in mind the old rule of poker: if you can't spot the fool at the table, then it's yourself

How can something be illegal?

There are ample ways for an activity or setup to be illegal. I don't say I'm always in agreement with the opinions of the lawmakers, but bare fact happens to be: governments have the guns and prisons, and neither you nor I do. Therefore, we had better stick with their interpretation of "right" and "wrong."

Allow me to have a look at one of the frequent offerings, which you will find in this or a very similar version anytime you just look around: it's the "network marketing" idea for partners (= you) to find investors, who then put their money into some type of investment, offered by a smart guy in Dubai who can be easily contacted by (only) some means of online messaging. The promised return of that investment is offered as 30% per month.

What can be bad about this offer – 30% is definitely better than any offer of your local credit union, isn't it?

Indeed, the 30 percent per month would be better than any savings account with a bank or credit union. If it were a return on investment, i.e. yield. And only if all investors would actually receive those payments. Both are quite questionable, as we should point out.

30% per month equals 360% per year even without taking into consideration compounding interests. I don't wish to shatter your illusions, but nobody can **guarantee or promise** that kind of yield, at least not in a stable currency. Any yield offered anywhere has to be earned by somebody producing and selling something – which brings us back to the question, how that is supposed to happen. Recall: If you can't find the fool at the table, you surely will find him in the mirror.

That said; let's dive a bit deeper into this purely hypothetical 30% offer.

First of all, it is an offer for an investment. Investment solicitors are heavily regulated in pretty much any major country. That means for you: either the initiator of this investment has registration and permit, or – you guessed it – he acts illegally. In case the initiator has an address outside the US, Canada, and the European Union, of course solely for tax reasons or because of the great weather there, you'll be fairly safe in assuming the initiator knows about it being a crime. Tax havens and tax loopholes are very well available inside this block of countries, and investment funds are for most part tax-exempt to begin with – exactly what is the initiator of this investment scheme doing outside your borders? Oh yeah – enjoying the great weather. Or the government's inability to get hold of him while there. Whichever ends first.

Why should you be bothered by the fact that the initiator is probably breaking the law? Well, if you referred customers/investors/fools to him, you have made a big splash into the grease pot:

1. You have referred an investment. To do so, you need a permit as a financial service provider or a regulated investment adviser – do you happen to have one? (I'd venture out assuming you don't and you won't get one, either)
2. You have aided somebody of whom you could have figured out without much effort the fact that he is a criminal. That makes you his accomplice – which is a crime, too
3. Did you yourself, by chance, collect monies and forward them to that guy? Did you in detail inform your clients about how specifically the money will be used for only legally permitted

activities? Maybe you just forgot to document this detailed information and have your client sign it? In that case, most likely you will be considered as having offered a direct investment yourself. I just hope you have your banking license still in the upper drawer of your desk – otherwise, you have committed yet another crime

4. You haven't referred any investor personally, instead you only signed up other persons who did provide the referrals – so you should be save, right? Wrong. All of your commissions are derived from the aforementioned illegalities, which means they are not commissions or profits at all – they are loot. So you will have to repay those and, on top of that, you are an accomplice in a conspiracy. Since nobody will deny you were actively working as part of a system incentivizing others to commit crimes, congratulation: you are now part of organized crime

All of that did sound attractive to you? In this case, I have a shipment of snow balls in hell that I could offer at a great discount, even a better discount in a package with some attractive ocean front property in Arizona or – if you prefer – some beach property at the Mediterranean Sea front of Switzerland.

Ok – no referrals to anonymous people in Dubai

Let's assume you have decided the thing with the prisons to be not the greatest idea on planet Earth. Consequently, you are trying to avoid clash with investment laws and financial services regulations.

You have moved on and are now looking at a different offer:

You're offered to participate in a network where you have to pay your sponsor a certain amount as compensation for her efforts to invite you in. As soon as you have signed up and paid, you are granted the permission to sponsor others into the network and collect money from them. This way, it takes only a few new partners to cover your total initial outlay, and from that point on you will enjoy all profit.

What else? Did you expect more information to follow? Not happening. Those "networks" really do exist, and still tons of people fall for them (oops, I should have issued a spoiler alert to warn you of my approaching opinion).

Why "fall for them"? Well, this structure is well known as "chain letter scam" – hardly anything happens besides you telling somebody to pay you money. Then this somebody can find somebody else to tell the same. In former times, this has been done by means of postal mail – hence the term.

Why is there a problem with those chain letter systems? It's simple, actually: no values are created by anybody for anybody. The entire thing is based on robbing the new ones and handing their money to the ones who were earlier. The "membership" you are buying is plain worthless because there is no ongoing business model. No service is provided, no product changes hands, and the only thing the membership entitles you to, is something you can do without that membership (namely, ask people for money).

Such chain letter schemes are, hardly surprising, illegal even without actual letters being involved. None of these systems does anything but rip off somebody to pay someone else. Consequently, they are all illegal. With one exception, though: the government's very own old age pension system (sometimes euphemistically called "Social Security") is working exactly that way and it's not illegal because the government made a law which says so. But Social Security, too, doesn't work – as evidenced by the many "reforms" and "loophole removals". Cynics tend to conclude from chain letters systems being illegal that the government doesn't wish competition.

How to spot a chain letter

In our everyday environment, chain letter systems commonly don't come with a warning label "Illegal chain letter" attached. What are the indications you are looking at such a system?

1. The company behind the network is not readily identifiable, cannot be reached, or doesn't provide contact information? You can't find out the legal representative of the company (who, in doubt, will be handed the legal papers from a court)? Keep your hands off!
2. Even before you figure out how and where the profits are produced, you are told "I am making $ xxx per day" or "minimum income of $ yyy per day." I don't care whether this amount is feasible or not. My point is, if you are self-employed, your income depends a good deal on your own performance (i.e. work,

at least in the early phases) – whoever fails to mention that explicitly, most likely forgets to mention other important facts, too

3. There are no or almost no goods (or value-producing services) which you could offer to anybody outside that network. That oftentimes is a pretty good indication of no values being generated at all

4. You are paying a high entry fee without detectable value you would get for it, or the assumed value only refers to documents usable internally in this very system – essentially nothing you could sell to end consumers to generate a profit from

5. If you are bringing a new partner into the network, you are receiving a payment (usually called commission) which is less than the new partner's payment for the entry fee (or those other worthless items)

6. The network is offering products or services, but those (or almost identical ones) are available in the marketplace for substantially less or even for free

7. This bullet point requires a bit calculation: take the amount of commissions you would receive for sales a new partner of yours would generate. To this commission amount, you add the commissions your personal sponsor will get for the very same sales of **your** partner. To that, you add the commissions paid to the sponsor of your sponsor for that very same sale. And maybe you go on and add the commissions paid to the sponsor's sponsor's sponsor, so you get the total commissions paid to 5 levels (sometimes called generations). Now have a look at that number and compare it to the sales price. Divide total commissions by the value of the sale. In retail, it's quite common for the retail price to include 60% for the retailers, wholesalers and for advertising (i.e., $60 for each $100 product price). As long as the total commissions paid in a marketing network don't excessively exceed these 60% (that means, commissions divided by product price is less than about 0.60), there is no problem. If, however, this percentage is substantially more (for example, 80% or even adding up to more than the product price itself), than alarm bells should be ringing in your head: no business can pay more commission than it makes in revenue minus its own costs. **No business**. NOPE (not on planet Earth)

I am aware that my list is a bit chunkier than the usual quick & easy "Identification Criteria" offered up by the diverse government entities around the globe. Let's compare the above list to a list published by "ScamWatch" of the Australian government:

"It is against the law to promote or participate in a pyramid scheme.

Warning signs

You are offered a chance to join a group, scheme, program, or team where you need to recruit new members to make money

The scheme involves offering goods or services of little or doubtful value that serve only to promote the scheme, such as information sheets

There are big up-front costs

The promoter makes claims like 'this is not a pyramid scheme' or 'this is totally legal'. "

Given the fact that specifically governments are operating the largest chain letter systems of all times (and because they are the only ones able to force us mere mortals into those systems; anybody else, even really evil criminals, still have to make us join voluntarily. The government, however, can force membership upon us by law and enforce it using their powers of seizing property and accounts, and by means of physical violence or threat thereof), we should be somewhat weary about what this governmental agency has to say. As the saying goes: he who sits in a house of glass will need a lot of glass cleaner.

Before we get to their first bullet point, we are already informed, "It is against the law to promote or participate in a pyramid scheme." The problem with this statement: it happens to be plain false.

Yes, I can guess what the author's intention had been when writing this sentence – but that doesn't improve anything. Whether or not a system can be presented in the image of a pyramid has nothing to do with this system, but a lot to do with your graphical presentation skills. Would you care for some rather simplistic examples?

How many parent couples do you have? Commonly only one, I would expect. Let's put that down on a little graphic.

How many children did those parents bring up? At least one (that would be you), maybe some more. Please write all of yourself and siblings below your parents, so you kids form a horizontal line – siblings should be besides each other.

Now you think of your own kids and the kids of your siblings, please. Write them below their respective parents: your children below yourself, your brother's children below your brother and so on.

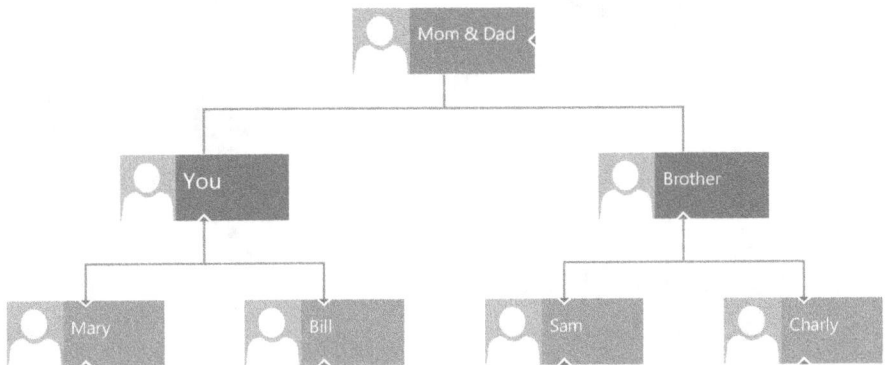

If you are an average family, what are you looking at right now on the paper in front of you? A pyramid. Oh – that's illegal, if you believe in the words of the Australian government.

Different example. Let's have a look at the school you have been attending when you were a kid: only one headmaster, below that person a bunch of teachers, below the teachers all their respective pupils... - what are we getting as visual representation? A pyramid. Uh-oh. School appears to be illegal, too. Would explain a lot, though.

How many CEOs does a company like GE have? Only one. How many members does their board of directors have? Currently 18. How many heads of lines of business are reporting to those? And how many department heads are below those? Team leaders? Employees? The further you progress, the wider the level spreads. How many customers does a company like that serve, compared to its number of employees? Even more.

It's fairly obvious: you are looking at a pyramid. Wow... this gotta be seriously illegal.

One last example to test whether the Australian government's Scam-Watch would consider it illegal:

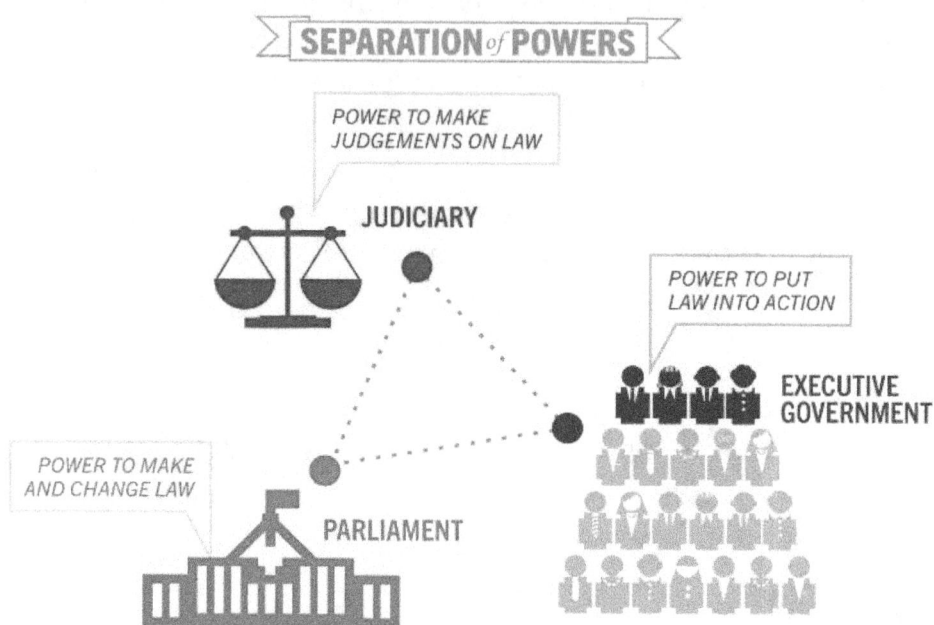

SEPARATION *of* POWERS

POWER TO MAKE JUDGEMENTS ON LAW

JUDICIARY

POWER TO PUT LAW INTO ACTION

EXECUTIVE GOVERNMENT

POWER TO MAKE AND CHANGE LAW

PARLIAMENT

Source of this image: Australia's Parliamentary Education Office.

This odd structure in the lower right corner looks awfully like... a pyramid! We did it; we managed to spot the illegal pyramid in the picture.

What's depicted there, by the way?

It's the Australian government's way of depicting the **Australian Executive Government**, therefore **itself**. Oops. Who knew?

Phrased differently: any given way of representing something graphically is **not** a suitable method of determining its legality. Regardless of how much a bureaucrat in an air-conditioned office building wishes life to be that clean cut.

Now we can proceed to ScamWatch's point A, already. That's where we learn how concerned we should be if you are supposed to invite other people into your system and that's the sole reason you are paid.

I very much assume the government's own army recruiters would fit the bill perfectly: they are working for the system with the sole purpose to bring new poor souls into it. Just as it works with recruiters of any kind – after all, that's their job. Therefore, it's also the only reason they are paid.

Again, we seem to have the problem that you cannot use a rather vague phrase to identify something as illegal or not illegal. Unless, of course, you would go so far and view a country's military as a fraudulent scheme – for which, from a certain point of view, you probably could make a case (new members enter the scheme based on intentional misrepresentations of facts; once you're in, it's quite difficult to get out of it even when you learn the truth; and all that with the added risk of ongoing damage to your health and life).

For a change, ScamWatch's point B actually has some meaningful advice in it – this roughly matches point 4 of my list, rolled out a bit earlier.

ScamWatch's point C, of course, is a source for fun and laughter: you're supposed to be suspicious if large upfront costs are due. Yeah, beloved bureaucrats, that tends to happen when you are going into business. If you want to break it down to this rather obvious criterion, pretty much every fast-food-franchise is at least halfway in prison. McAlcatraz, so to say.

Nope, the world outside your governmental hallways is not that simple. Real life for a business person is by far less pleasant than politicians and bureaucrats seem to think it is. For a good part not despite but because of the works of offices like those. However, you could argue several million dollars aren't large sums of money for a government employee.

Finally, ScamWatch's point D is a poster child of uselessness: "The promoter makes claims like 'this is not a pyramid scheme' or 'this is totally legal'."

Ok, let me get that straight. If an evildoer is asked whether or not his (illegal) scheme is legally acceptable, what will he answer? Of course, he will tell you it's totally legal. So far, ScamWatch got that right. But here, their logic ends – since the evil guys are responding "It is totally legal", everybody claiming such must be promoting something illegal, right?

What exactly, in their opinion, is somebody supposed to say if he **does** offer something completely legal and acceptable – such as a doctor offering a flu shot? You ask the doc "But is this legal?" – now, what would he answer? "Of course it is completely legal; otherwise I wouldn't be offering it." **Hah**... gotcha! ScamWatch has warned us about those guys! They claim it to be totally legal because they are scoundrels and we are about to be scammed.

Ok, so that's ridiculous. But what else is somebody expected to answer when asked for the legality of his offering **and** he is actually offering something indeed legal? Maybe something like "Normally, I would have to say it is perfectly legal. But since the scammers are claiming this all the time, I now have to tell you I am trying to defraud you – in order to make you believe me it's legal?" or what is the idea of ScamWatch's list writer(s)?

"Are you lying?"

　　　"No."

"You are a liar!"

Makes for a great sketch on TV – but leads nowhere in reality.

Knee-jerk pamphlets like this government publication can't be the base for a real decision-making process for you or anybody else threatened by the flood of fraudulent attacks all around us.

We won't get around the need of kicking those silly lists into the bin and start thinking for ourselves.

Next, I would like to spend some minutes, together with you, working through another aspect of the "That's fraud" judgement. There are way too many fraudsters out there; you can't just frustratedly look at the outrageously useless government writings and then skip any real protection against rip-offs.

On the other hand, there are actually legit business models out there which are indeed viable and which you could use to get your own self-employment off the ground; the need to differentiate the bad apples from the others is common to all types of business models, not just network marketing.

Not to mention the fact that there is a multitude of statistics desperately trying to make sure you can't see the difference between the two.

Whenever you will put this book aside and move on with your life, I would be happy if this could be the one point you are taking with you. Let's get to it.

That's a total scam!

About half a year ago, I had the questionable honor to attend (but not participate in) a conversation between a just starting network marketing sponsor, who happened to be a friend of mine (yes, you can actually have some of those guys as friends!), and a man who previously had indicated he was looking for a business opportunity.

I am presenting this brief conversation here with the words of the interested man put in **bold** and providing some of my annotations in [brackets].

"Actually, I am looking for some way to make money. But don't dare to suggest network marketing or any other such pyramid schemes."

"Will be difficult, I guess; recently, you mentioned you have problems with you spinal column and the discs, which is why you cannot work regular hours of any meaningful duration. You can't do office work, and physical labor like construction or warehouse doesn't cut it for you, either..."

"True, but network marketing is all a big scam"

[At this point, the just-starting sponsor is about to simply end the conversation and forget about that prospect. Surprisingly, though, he first wants to know where this opinion came from]

"If I may ask – have you previously been involved with a network marketing business, or where did your strong emotions come from?"

"Yes, I had something in the past. But, as I'm telling you, that's all fraud and rip-off."

[But here definitely the sponsor has mentally given up on the hope to help the prospect with a new business start. However, now he himself wants to know, which network might have caused such a bad reaction – if only to avoid this one in the future himself]

"What type of network are we talking about? Have you been a customer with them, or did you get involved with distributing their products?"

[A sensible question because a distributor's point of view is of course completely different than a customer's point of view]

"No, I was a sales guy. And let me tell you, that's all a rip-off. Total scam. We have sold phone contracts which scammed the people."

"I see, so the contracts were the scam in your opinion. That wasn't clear to me, thanks for clarifying this a bit"

"Yeah, we sold the contracts to elderly people who usually don't read the fine print. As long as they don't use the phone much, our contracts are indeed cheaper than the competition. But once they started to be on the phone for an extended period of time, that's when it got really expensive. Total fraud, I tell you."

"Ah, I understand"

[Here I have to remark something to you, dear reader: What we have learnt from the ex-phone-contract-salesperson is interesting. So far, he didn't present a single aspect where you could see the network company doing anything fraudulent or even unethical. However, what does qualify as potentially fraudulent, is his (the ex-salesperson's) own method to sell those contracts.

Instead of working through the effort to evaluate his products strength's and so-called "use cases", and then approach matching customers on the base of his analysis, he took the easy route and tried to push those contracts to presumably naïve elderly people; he has forgotten to mention his offer's drawbacks and apparently didn't know the advantages – so we can assume he didn't provide much real service to anybody.

Actually, such strange contracts with extremely low base fee and very high costs per minute phone usage do have their uses and make perfect sense for some customers – specifically for those who want to have such a phone but do not intend to use it for outgoing calls. In order to figure that out, however, one would need to work out contract details as well as the customers' needs]

[Back to our little question & answer session]

"Was this scammy behavior limited to the contracts, or did your network scam you as well, with commission payments or the like?"

„What?"

"I mean to ask, were the commission calculations correct and did you get paid on time?"

„How would I know? I haven't sold much – I don't want to sell something like that! "

[Ah… we're closing in on the problem. The ex-salesman unfortunately didn't sell anything – means: he didn't manage to close any deals. That of course is bad for a sales person, no matter what specifically he is trying to sell. It's understandable he doesn't want to admit to himself that he could be part of the problem. Wisely, our sponsor here decides not to add insult to injury]

"Makes sense, I get that. In that case, you wouldn't know if the network company was also taking advantage of their distributors. But if you didn't sell anything because understandably you refused to sell those contracts, what did constitute your really bad experience with the company – aside from not making money, which is bad enough?"

"I told you, this stuff is total fraud. Because of that, they seized my bank account. My assets frozen, sent me into a downwards spiral. I tell you: never again!"

[Now, that sparked my interest: how can he end up with a frozen bank account if nothing has been sold and he left the network soon after he started? There are only very few entities who can freeze or seize your accounts, and network marketing organizations are not amongst those. That aside, networks collect their fees before anything happens – there is no opportunity for anything to be seized, to begin with. Leaves me with only one suspicion…]

"Seized accounts? How did the network get to seize your bank account?"

„No, not the network. The IRS"

[Yeah, that was my suspicion. Alas, if the IRS or other revenue department made the grab, then I would dare to claim: some pieces of information are missing here. The sponsor picked up on that as well, so he asks for clarification]

"Why the IRS? My understanding was that you didn't have any sales and certainly no profits to pay taxes for?"

„I didn't. They simply assessed it that way. "

"What do you mean – they simply assessed? Didn't you file a tax return stating the facts?"

„Nobody told me to file a tax return with that stuff on it. After a few years, they seized my account out of the blue."

[Aaaah… after a few years, not earlier? In that case, the IRS was quite patient with him. When the IRS seizes accounts despite him not having earned anything, then it has estimated his income beforehand. That, in turn, does happen only after the taxpayer didn't file the return despite several reminders. In other words, the self-proclaimed victim has completely ignored all reminders sent to him in sequence, probably justifying that behavior to himself with the logic that he didn't have any income for which to pay taxes. Question, however, would be: how would the IRS know you don't have income unless you actually tell them?]

"Oh – so, you didn't send in tax returns and the IRS then decided to guesstimate. Yeah, obviously those estimates never end up in your favor."

"Yeah, robbers. I didn't know I had to file the tax return for the business."

[To be clear at this point: that was a plain lie. The IRS **did** send him letters stating by which dates he had to file which return – and even reminded him of the upcoming due dates. He admitted as much in a later conversation; nevertheless, he still insists nobody told him he had to file a tax return.

Further: he didn't have to file a separate tax return for his business – instead, in his case, that would have been part of his personal tax return. Which he didn't file, either]

"Well, that's a burden we all have to bear, isn't it?"

„But nobody told me. And this phone company not telling me, that's real intentional fraud!"

[And this point, we are leaving this conversation – I don't want to bore you to death]

I believe it has become clear with how much past history and encumbrances the entire topic of network marketing has been burdened for this poor guy. That, however, had little to do with the network company being fraudulent, or even with products being questionable. They still might be, but that was not the problem he had faced.

His failure had much more to do with himself trying to not sell anything but making money as quick as possible without having put much effort into it. Nice try, but the outcome was somewhat predictable. He would have experienced a similar result with about every other business, regardless of network marketing or not.

He getting into trouble with the department of revenue is a result of not filing a tax return and choosing to ignore any and all reminders from the government; that is hardly a responsibility of the network – for tax returns, every individual is responsible on his/her own. That doesn't change when you join a network organization. So, his issues are the result of his decision to live in an imagined world of self-deception and make-believe. Whenever reality collides with this dream world, the man caught in the middle develops clinical depression and slides down a spiral right into the middle of a huge pile of problems.

That, however, is well known among self-employed persons and their psychiatrists – at least if they are part of the 60% to 95% of startup businesses which don't survive the first 5 years. The end result besides financial ruin is almost always a kind of psychological bankruptcy.

As disappointing and unpleasant that may be – it's not an attribute of network marketing and certainly it's not any type of fraud, therefore quite unsuitable as an aid to decide for or against one or another network business, or any other business, for that matter.

Still, we must find a way to uncover fraudsters and scoundrels – which is why, when confronted with such "experiences" with network marketing fraud or "MLM-rip-offs", you have to insist on asking and finding out the real core of the respective experience.

Whenever someone has such deep-seated hate for network marketing (or anything else, really), that person has gone through painful experiences. But for you, dear reader, only cases are of value that actually are related to the network company itself, to their products, their behavior, their compensation plan or their way of doing business. The

IRS or Department of Revenue is nothing you will get away from; neither will you be able to evade the necessity for investing your own labor into your business and roll up your sleeves.

If, after a while of talking, this "It's a total scam" turns out to indicate that the person somehow expected to get rich over night without any own actual involvement – then that person has confused self-employment with a lottery. As soon as seized accounts show up in the story line **without criminal charges**, you may safely assume to see causes unrelated to the network company and very much related to the person trashing all the mail from the government.

By the way – the problem described by the "prospect" (that IRS issue) is the main reason I insist: if you are starting a business, do so only with a CPA (certified public accountant) at hand. If necessary, you need to find the money for the CPA.

No way around that.

Nobody is immune to the severe emotional roller coaster rides triggered by letters from the IRS or any other taxation authority. That's because they are designed to have that effect!

If you have a CPA, those letters go to him rather than you – and he then can tell you the IRS's desires in much friendlier words. He knows all the little evil phrases they are using and can shield you against their consequences by simple objecting to them or correcting the "mistakes" of IRS agents. All that without you getting involved at all. That alone is worth every single penny, even if those CPA fees are painful in the beginning.

Again, that is true for every type of income-producing activity. Nevertheless, your duty is making money, not the wrecking of your nerves.

Training your eyes

Let's examine some real examples and see how well you are able to spot the issues.

Case 1: found by referral

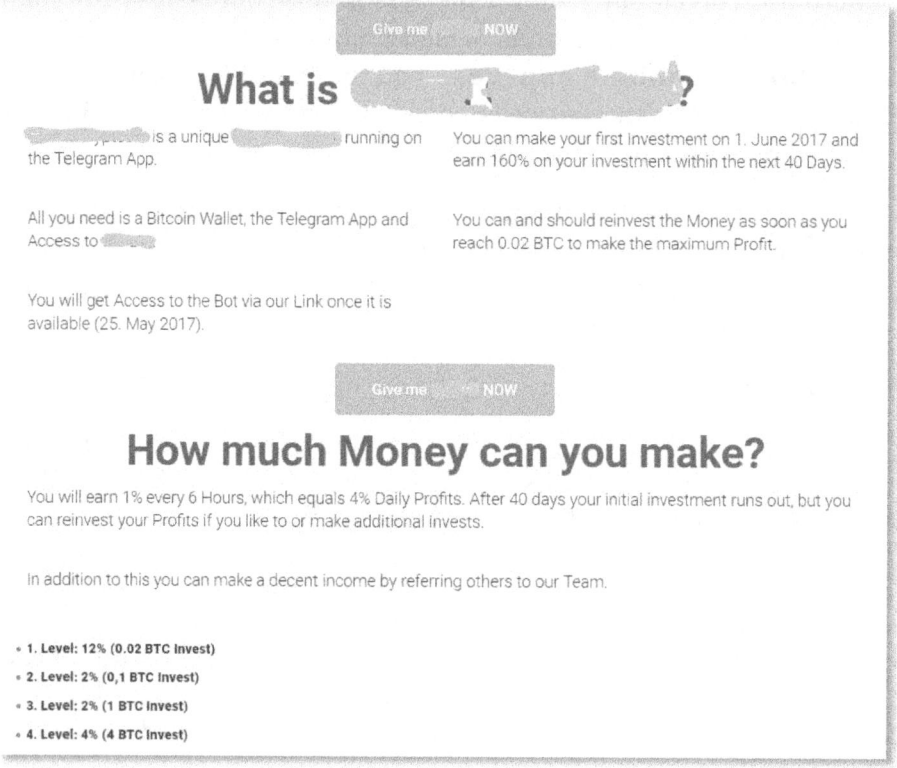

I took the liberty to blur the promoter and "product" names – at this stage, it's about the offer itself.

What do we get to know? Not that much, it appears. We don't get to know how we are supposed to make money – only **that** we apparently are promised a fixed yield.

We cannot see how we could create value for anybody (more value than would exist without us), but we are told we would earn 160% within 40 days. We are told that our initial investment runs out after 40 days, but we are free to reinvest profits and/or make additional investments. In other words, whatever you invest will be locked up for 40 days – that's really all it says.

Further, we get to know this is some kind of multi-level-system – because different commission percentages are applied to different levels, adjacent to the information that we can make a decent living by referring others to the team. Once you have looked around and didn't find anything those percentages could be referring to, you are probably aware that those percentages don't mean much without someone telling you what those percentages are based on.

Last, but not least, we learn that you can start with as little as 0.02 BTC; currently, that's equivalent to about 60 US$.

If you want to get more information about this system, you are invited to click on one of those links, which bring you to a page saying essentially the same, just with more words and more hype. No additional information to be had. Well, none about the system, that is. But they do tell you how to get in touch with them – by means of a messenger application, which you first have to download and install on your computer or smartphone. Only then will you be able to exchange messages with the organizers.

I assume it didn't take much effort for you to see all the problems with this fantastic opportunity. Here are a few obvious ones:

Whoever creates advertising text (aka ad copy) like that, probably never bothered to read any relevant laws, it appears. If you click on one of the links with the expectation of obtaining more information about the initiator/operator of this network – not going to happen. You may contact an anonymous person at an unknown place on Earth using a messenger software. Legal "about us," phone number or even just an email address? Well, no. Name and address of the legally responsible person? Not today, sorry.

And yes, you did read that correctly: you are expected to install somebody else's software on your machine in order to just exchange text messages with those guys and gals. From my own experience as a software developer I can tell you: pretty bad idea.

You are expected to trust somebody about their software being safe and sound, about it not injecting tons of viruses and worms into your PC or smartphone – but they in turn don't trust you enough to give you direct contact opportunity without first having to install foreign software? I don't know about you, but to me that sounds more than just questionable.

The ad text promises 100% automated income for you. So, not only do they vaguely suggest that you wouldn't need to do anything – they are advertising it explicitly.

Since there is no work to be done (apart from the small spot in all that beauty, namely that you have to surrender control of your PC or phone to somebody else whom you never have seen or spoken to), it remains unclear why you are expected to pay anything into this system. After all, at 4% yield per day, they must be earning so much money that your 60 bucks hardly can make any difference, right? Speaking of – the 4% promise is definite, too. There are no "up to" or other phrases like it, instead: it's a fixed 4% you are told you will receive.

Reading that text gives the feeling of playing kind of "bingo for law breakers": pretty much each line of text gives you the opportunity to check off another broken law on your bingo card. He who checked off every law on his card, wins. Or something like that.

You are offered an investment – that alone violates a whole slew of laws and regulations, for which the SEC (in the US) is the appropriate watchdog. Other countries have their own version of it.

You are promised astronomical 4% per **day** – which is as explosive as a land mine. This yield is so absurd that, according to the legal system, it must have been obvious to you: this can't be for real. Therefore, you are not a victim; instead, you become the perpetrator. Whether accessory to crime or an accomplice – those are just semantic details. Fact is: this offer is so outlandish; you **knowingly** participate in a scam as soon as you do participate at all.

On top of that, most jurisdictions have an upper limit of any type of fixed yield (which bears all the hallmark of interests, regardless how it is called). Some US states have a cap at 12%, some at 18%, Germany has 20% - but those numbers are **per year**, not per day or month. If you now think you at least had a claim against the organizers for the 4% per day, even if you don't do anything else – think twice. The law for most part says: there is a cap of 20% (or 12 or 18), and you are charging more than that – ergo your claim is null and void.

Matter-of-factly, it won't matter much if or if not you are guilty of usury (interest overcharge) under the aforementioned rules. Fact is, you will get any payment just long enough to keep you bringing more victims into the system.

As soon as the stream of new fools starts drying up, there will be nobody to take those absurd amounts from – and next thing you know is the Attorney General clawing back all amounts ever paid to you, in order to repay those amounts to the real victims (and to the office of the Attorney General, not necessarily in this order).

But, you say, the 4% isn't absurd, at least not to you? Let's do a little bit of basic math: the ad text explicitly states you have to contribute **at least** 0.02 Bitcoin. And they do mention you are welcome to invest more than the minimum **and** to re-invest the yield earned. From the 4% they offer, it sounds very much like you are encouraged to pay more into it. Why not play sheep and do just that, at least with pen and paper? We will assume you transfer 1 Bitcoin to them and we opt to re-invest the yield everyday back into the system. Whenever something is paid back, you re-invest it immediately (the text explicitly invites us to do precisely that).

Now, you can see the Bitcoin (BTC) amount grow happily ever after – until you notice something odd happening on day 431. That day is barely more than 14 months into the future; therefore we aren't talking about some mythical day past the end of the world, right? Waiting 14 months is not a big deal when we get it sweetened with 4% per day – would you agree?

Yeah – **we** can wait 14 months. Alas, this system cannot. What does our account show on day 431? It claims 21,102,597 BTC, therefore 21 million 102 thousand 597 Bitcoin. It's a large number, but then – the daily yield is remarkably high.

Why do I have a problem with specifically day 431, which appears not all that much different from any other day?

Very simple – it's the day of truth.

The Bitcoin crypto-currency system is designed in a way that mathematically guarantees: there will never be more than 21 million Bitcoins in the universe. Never ever. This limit is mathematically integrated into the Bitcoin logic, and while the total number of BTC can (and does) come closer to that number day by day, the speed of approaching the limit gets less and less. Every step closer to the 21 million limit is much more difficult than the previous step, and in order to reach that limit itself, a mathematical equation of infinite complexity would have to be solved. "Infinite" means just that. Not "very high" or "incredibly high," but infinite.

By definition, our planet doesn't have the capacity for infinite complex equations – so this 21 million barrier can never be reached (much less exceeded). It's similar to the speed of light in physics, where no matter particle can ever reach the speed of light because it would require an infinite amount of energy to do it. However, while the speed-of-light thing is still a hypothesis (albeit a well thought-through one), the 21-million-limit of Bitcoin is mathematical fact.

Then how can you have more than 21 million BTC in your account on day 431 almost effortlessly?

The solution by now should be obvious: you cannot. Any system promising you just that with Bitcoins can be one thing and one thing only. I don't need to spell out the term "fraud," do I?

Would the ad text have said something of paying you the equivalent in some other currency, in that case the whole thing would have just been "most likely impossible." But by clearly stating that you are to receive the 4%/day yield in Bitcoins, which you may leave there to compound, the text tells us something else, too: somebody does not intend to make good on that promise. Which would explain the lack of legal contact information and the glaring impossibility to legally enforce any claims against the organizers.

Oh – you still are really considering participation and just getting out before it's too late? Think twice... even the participation and promotion is most likely a criminal act.

And don't forget, my calculation was based on your 1 BTC investment. You **alone** would bring that house of cards to collapse within 14 months. Make that 50 people trying the same "get out just in time" approach, and you have a pretty good idea why there are so many of those Bitcoin get-rich-quick schemes. They hardly can get older than 4 weeks before they are shut down or collapsed.

It's just strange that still so many people get themselves into these things – greed eating brain, I would say. Or maybe desperation eating brain. Either way, mathematics still applies.

An important clarification

I myself do not have a problem with Bitcoin – on the contrary. The idea is fascinating – means of payment which cannot be manipulated by a government or central bank. A currency of which everybody up-front is aware of the built-in limit of 21 million units. Hyper-inflation impossible. Now, that doesn't guarantee any exchange rate or any value. All it does is guarantee that no government can print additional currency units at their leisure, thereby stealing value from owners of existing currency units.

I, too, have so-called Bitcoin miners (computers) working for me, which function similar to the gold diggers way back when in California. Also, I am the developer of one of the faster bitcoin-mining programs for PCs.

However, for mining bitcoins, nobody needs anonymous organizations, which demand a payment in return for strange promises of absurd yields. Anybody can mine Bitcoins today by just using a computer with a strong multiprocessor core and a matching software. You would be doing the mining entirely for your own wallet – neither promote it nor sign up for some scam; simply do it. Then it's even legal.

Recently I have been told, *"I can't figure out why you aren't signing up with us and invest in Bitcoin. You're a bright guy, it should be obvious how much profit you can make!"*

At this point, we need to discriminate between "invest in Bitcoin" and "sign up with us." The latter has nothing to do with investing in Bitcoin. You can simply go out and buy some Bitcoin in exchange for the market value in dollars or any other major currency. The other part, the "sign up with us", well… that's what this book is about. Never ever confuse an investment speculation with an organization pushing it.

If you buy Bitcoin in expectation of a higher value at a later time, then you are speculating. This is completely ok, not much different from buying a piece of contemporary art, hoping for a later rise of the market price.

It is perfectly ok for you to speculate on price movements of almost anything. You are allowed to do it, and there are usually even sections of the tax law telling you how the tax on those profits will be calculated.

However, whenever an organization is trying to talk a speculation into some type of guaranteed yield, income, or even into a safe place for your money – run!

Case 2: Incomprehensible?

From my news stream on the blue social network comes the following text, augmented by a picture of gold bullion:

"HELLO YOU PURE GOLD GO TO 1GR. A 100gr.
  SAPPI THREE THINGS YOU CAN MONET WITH THESE GOLD THEN YOU CAN SELL THE COMPANY YOU CAN LEAVE IT OR YOU CAN LEAVE A COST OF CABLES 'CLEAR THAT THE COMPANY IS DESIGNED !!
  AND YOU CAN MAKE 7000 $ BEN AND THAT WHEN YOU WANT!
  FOR INFO IN PRIVATE THANK YOU!"

I didn't make any changes – it's still as unreadable as it has been from the beginning. If I were thinking positively, I could come to believe the originator intended to create some kind of word art.

Truth being told, I am not much of a positive thinker – so, I don't go with the word artist idea and instead believe such assumption would give the ad's text writer way too much credit.

At least it's some consolation that no other reader has responded to this unbeatable offer, either.

Case 3: Speaking personally

Same source as the previous one, but different date:

"Who here is looking for a top online company where you can invest your funds profitably and fear-free? Please get in touch! Pn pls."

You can get in touch with the person via said social network – at least you have to give him that. Since we are expected to write to him directly, we can even assume he will be reading the messages; this, too, is far beyond what is frequently found in this industry.

Alas, the problem-free zone ends here. For you as a reader of this book, the issues are easily identifiable, aren't they?

Right: our old friends – conflicts with the laws regulating investment advice, which is clearly stated "…can invest your funds…"; all that as an ad without being asked personally. If he would have dispensed information after explicitly being asked for it by somebody, things (in some jurisdictions) might look different. But this way – no chance. Investment, profitably, fear-free – that's a combination of terms you don't want to read unless you are dealing with a registered investment adviser or a bank or broker.

Case 4: the moderate newspaper ad

"Are you looking for a mini-job, are open and communicative, like to talk with people? You want easy additional $450 per month? Call me today Phone (xxx) xxx-xxxx"

A call to that phone number then reveals a friendly woman at the other end of the line, who would like to win us as new partners in a network marketing system. At least she says so. We had to ask explicitly 3 times, but hey – at least she mentioned it at all.

Why do I have a problem with it being a network marketing opportunity? Because the advertisement is offering something clearly different: in unambiguous letters, the ad copy asks whether you are looking for a "mini-job." Regardless of what specifically constitutes a mini-job, in everyday language, a "job" refers to a contract of employment and **not** to a self-employed business. The amount mentioned (those $450) don't just give randomly the impression you could earn that money, but probably is intended to look like a more or less fixed salary, again: enforcing the image of a salaried employment rather than of a self-responsible business situation.

We don't get to know from the ad the line of business they are in or how the money is to be generated – for that reason, I am not making a judgement about the viability of the network opportunity or the legitimacy of the network company itself. But I will give you my opinion about the method used by the advertiser. "Bait and switch under false flag".

If you encounter something like that, get away from it as soon as possible. Who starts off by telling you only half or none of the truth will be unlikely to change this habit later in the game. Do you really want to work with somebody like that? I don't necessarily assume bad intentions (well... the temptation is big), but if your sponsor isn't able to tell a job from self-employment, then he isn't worth much as mentor. Nor as a sponsor.

How does No-Fraud look like?

Recalling the conversation with the ex-salesguy for phone contracts, we have seen there are cases of terrible experiences that have little or nothing to do with fraud or scam. From my experience, this group is actually larger than the group of real fraud victims.

Looking at the large pool of all failed attempts, I believe we can subdivide the cases in three main categories:

- A. Systemic fraud, where the system itself was never intended to produce any real profits – instead, the plan from the get-go has been to extract money from newcomers and use it to pay existing members and, most importantly, the original organizers
- B. The newbie has been introduced into the system under false pretext or false flag, if you will. Terms and facts have been misrepresented or the salesperson/sponsor did lie outright – similar to what you would expect from politicians during election campaigns. Or from car manufacturers when publishing the specifications of emissions and fuel consumption for their car's engines
- C. The newbie himself has caused the failure by means of his own behavior (or lack thereof), as in case of the ex-phone-salesperson

Overlap between the cases is possible and commonly happens; the by far most relevant group with negative experiences seems to be an overlap of groups B and C.

While there are indeed ample group-A-cases, meaning intentional fraud already at the system level, those numbers pale in face of the huge number of group B or C cases.

Since you want to find out about the real story presented to you, first you should try to figure out whom you are talking to. Is it somebody victimized in a group A case, one from group B or is that person guilty under group C – after all, group C candidates are not victims, they are perpetrators (you could also call them masochists, since they themselves are for most part their only victim).

If you have a group-C-representative in front of you, pretty much nothing is relevant to you when trying to build an opinion about a specific network marketing company and its suitability for you. All you will hear from that person most likely ends up being accusations, finger pointing and perfectly logical sounding explanations why everything is somebody else's fault.

Now, if that person happens to be a close friend of yours, of course you will continue to listen. However, you shouldn't expect any serious insights that could help your evaluation.

Group A is of course important, but much less so than you may expect. Taking the strange 4%-per-day Bitcoin investment offer as an example, it's easy to see why: you on your own can make the fraud collapse in no later than 14 months with a very moderate investment. Those so-called "Bitcoin MLMs" don't have just one member, for inexplicable reasons they commonly have several thousands, bringing the inevitable crash much closer to home than those 14 months. Frequently, they don't even survive 30 days. Which means: by the time you get to know about systemic fraud, that specific scam is already long gone – and something else took its place (not seldom with the same organizers, even the same promoters, and oftentimes with sentences like "yeah, we in the industry saw that collapse coming, which is why we didn't promote it for the longest time. But now we have one, which is the real deal! Sign up now for a huge profit!") Therefore, by the time someone tells you about a really fraudulent system, there is usually no chance you could ever sign up with it: it simply doesn't exist anymore. Word-of-mouth nowadays is slower than scams collapse.

As I see it, the largest problem is with group B. This, unfortunately, doesn't distinguish group B from any other sales person being more creative than appropriate. Whenever the one-time sales commission becomes more important than the ongoing customer relationship, factual data tends to become a bit blurry.

With that, I mean: the sales person gets more or less minor details wrong or makes them up while he speaks. "Minor details" according to the opinion of the sales person, of course. You as the victim might have a different view.

Technical data or attributes tend to be created on the fly without the manufacturer knowing about it, known disadvantages and risks tend to somehow not get mentioned at all, clear questions all too commonly are "misunderstood". Properties are assured which the product doesn't have and which are not even planned for the future of this product.

These sales habits are well-known and are mostly associated with insurance sales agents or used car salesmen. As a matter of fact, those people can be found in every industry and anywhere you look for them. They are the people who don't know any other way of selling. So, they resort to a behavior you could call "creative persuasion" or just "plain lying".

We all are aware of cases when bank employees or credit brokers have "skipped" essential parts of the consulting session they are required to perform – and instead have replaced it with flogging the victim their product. Court records are full of that stuff. A relationship of trust has been abused to provide a false sense of safety – of which the bank or the broker knew full well how misplaced it had been. The respective banks and "consultants" have sometimes been forced to compensate their victims or pay fines, but that won't repair the damage done to their clients' trust.

Exactly the same issue exists when a network sponsor is pulling a friend or relative into a network marketing system under false flags: the sponsor may legally get away with it because it's nearly impossible to afterwards prove what the sponsor did or did not say. The damage to the trust, however, remains. Who's doing business that way usually has very few friends and almost no relatives still talking to him.

Even more often than this gross neglect we can encounter situations where an actually well-meaning sponsor is confronted with questions for which he doesn't have an answer. Sometime back in our childhood, we have learnt: if you don't know the answer, you are worth less than others are, and you are probably stupid. Both are bad. So, instead of admitting to not knowing something, we make up whatever sounds reasonable enough to fit into the picture. Upon the next such question, we need to come up with another small invented item that fits the bill. Then another one, which should fit everything we said so far.

The right answer would have been to say: I don't know, but let's find out.

Usually, the ego is too large for this response – and that's why a sponsor easily ends up on the wrong path.

The problem with those incorrect answers grows with the magnitude of their consequences.

If a buddy wants to sell you a book, he probably will recommend it. Now, totally surprising to him, you ask whether it's written in your language. If your buddy now would admit he doesn't know, that also would uncover his recommendation as pretty much worthless because he himself didn't read it.

So, at this point, he has the option to say that he doesn't know – and paddle back on the recommendation. If he chooses to not do so, he will have to tell you something he himself doesn't know – and then hope for the best.

You then order the book, just to figure out that your knowledge of Kisuaheli might not be sufficient to understand a single word inside that book. Your confidence in the buddy's book recommendation might take a hit, but other than that, the damage probably will be somewhat limited.

However, if you were talking about a 20-issue encyclopedia with one book coming into your home per week, the damage will be larger. Not only is the monetary loss larger, on top of that you will be reminded of your untrustworthy buddy once a week for the next 20 weeks.

The problem with half-truths and misrepresentations in the context of network marketing happens to be the miniscule issue about you just starting a whole new part of your future, based on the self-employed activity within this network. The consequences of lies in this situation are plenty and very long-lasting...

This brings us directly to a related issue with group B cases: you as a potential new member are not entirely innocent. What is offered to you is not a beverage or a book – it's a business model. If you can't be bothered to dig into details and get all information required, then you are at least partially an accomplice. As the saying goes: there are no victims, just volunteers. Sounds harsh, I know. But it's true.

When you venture out to buy a new car, every dealer will assume you are going to take care of the legal requirements like driver's license and liability insurance. The driver's license certainly is not a problem for which the dealer could be held responsible.

When buying an airplane ticket, one would assume you are taking care of anything related to your destination on your own. Whether you actually want to go there at all, for example. Or whether your passport is still valid, if it is an international destination. Sure, the agency or airline will probably give you a short check list to assist – but it's your own responsibility to read this list and make sure everything is fine.

The same is even truer in case of a business model, which you plan to use. Or a network you want to join. It can be assumed that you are bringing at least a modicum of own interest to the table.

How does a Network Marketing Company look like?

It takes two to tango, and network marketing is no different. The two parts of the model are the manufacturer (or brand name owner), whose products are supposed to be sold – we call that company the "network company." The other part is the sales organization, consisting of many many many self-employed people. This organization we will call the "network," which should come as no surprise.

In traditional company structures the sales network consists of licensed dealerships (the car dealership system works like that), or the manufacturer uses independent distribution channels with rather loose ties to the manufacturer (the wholesales/distributor model). The network marketing model is closer to the model of licensed dealership, but comes with its own special aspects.

Main difference between the model with licensed dealership and the network marketing model is the territory protection granted to a licensed dealer – and the lack of such protective features in network marketing.

As a result, if Bob owns a dealership, he will do whatever it takes to prevent a newcomer from opening up a car dealership for the same car maker anywhere close to Bob's place of business. Preferably, Bob would like to see you not at all in his industry (car sales).

In case of network marketing, things are quite the opposite: not only are new members of the sales organization accepted by existing ones, actually signing up new members is explicitly part of the core strategy. This way, the network companies are using most customer's inherent desire to buy at a discount, no matter how justified the retail price may be.

This behavior of customers is pretty much precisely what I have experienced for myself as a young man when repeatedly buying the latest computer hardware components, and frequently entire computer systems. To save some money, I registered a business claiming to do computer retail – and then went on to present this documentation to computer part wholesalers. That yielded lower prices for me than I would have had to pay otherwise.

Did that turn me into a retailer? Not really, no.

Did my business fail because I never generated any profits? No, it hasn't been a real business to begin with. I just wanted to buy at a discount, and this goal has been accomplished.

Please keep this description of my "computer business" in mind when looking at the network marketing model.

As example, we'll look at a network selling skin care products. Let's assume my friend Alice is enthusiastic about those products and wants to buy them on a regular base. What recommendation would I give?

Clear-cut case: try to sign up as distribution partner – then you can buy those products at a substantial discount.

Are the network members happy about people joining for the sole reason of buying for their own consumption? Well, I'd think they would prefer to see some more sales initiative from Alice (which Alice won't be providing because that never was her intention). Will the network kick her out because of that? Hardly.

Why am I so sure about that?

As soon as you join a network marketing organization, you will be assigned a mentor (often called "sponsor"); this sponsor from then on will receive a small commission whenever you order something from the network company. This commission is intended to incentivize the mentor for his help provided to you and for him being available to answer your questions.

In case of Alice, there will be no questions – just product orders. How much effort will that be for her sponsor? Zero. The sponsor will get paid a little for doing nothing – hard to beat, I'd say.

Actually, a large number of members in those sales organizations in reality are simply end users of the products who wanted to buy at a discount. Nothing wrong with that, from the network company's point of view. That's the company producing the goods, and their main wish is to increase sales.

To keep frustration of the "real" sales people regarding the "fake members" at bay, most network marketing organizations are offering incentives for sponsors who are signing up such under-cover retail customers. As the network company sees it, it doesn't matter much whether it is selling to would-be retailers or real end-users of the products – the difference in prices would have gone to the sales organization anyway. To keep the retail organization happy, the network company simply offers up those incentives to make up for a part of the lost profits that should have come from the retail customers (which are now posing as retailers themselves).

Traditional sales organizations are aiming at large sales volumes generated by as few as possible retail partners (true for cars, washing machines and the like).

Network marketing systems are using the approach to work with a huge number of retail partners, each of which needs to sell only small numbers. Sometimes, even very small numbers are sufficient.

Both models are doomed to generate enough sales in order to produce sufficient revenue and profits for survival of the producing company as well as the sales organization – that's an economic necessity and completely independent of the organizational structure. This aspect, however, seems to frequently get lost on members of a network marketing organization.

Now it is true, you don't need to generate all sales by yourself, nor are you able to. Regardless, somebody needs to generate the sales – you do it yourself, or you need to find somebody who does. If you don't manage to do either, your business is a failure. As easy as that. Unless you didn't want to make money and only intended to buy at a discount – but that is not a business anyway, in my book.

The traditional model (say, car dealership) calls for employees and referrers (called bird scouts) doing this work for their boss. In a network marketing system, the sales are done by the partners who you could win to sign up with you (those partners are called "the downline" in the network industry).

Let me repeat that: Completely independent of the model's structure, without sufficient sales you won't be successful in the long run. Mathematics has a tendency of getting in the way of anybody who believes otherwise.

Next, we'll have a look at the mechanisms used by those organizations.

Network mechanics

This chapter is dedicated to the tactics commonly used by network marketing organizations to achieve their goals. This should prove helpful since that's an area where most networks are using similar methods and structures.

The most notable attribute of the network organization clearly is its composition of a huge army of individual soldiers, militarily speaking. Every sales partner is an individual, self-employed person – not an employee, and not a boss, either. It's important to keep this in mind because that also implies all those independent sales people have the same problems as every other self-employed solopreneur, namely:

- They usually are not exactly great at organizing their time
- They often have not set any goals to aim at, much less intermediate milestones to check their success against
- They haven't come up with a strategy and didn't produce a written plan
- They postpone unpleasant or boring tasks right to the point in time when this procrastination blows up in their face and causes a catastrophe
- For most part, their only means of making a sale is: lower the price

Psychologists and long-time business owners agree in that point: all those points are problems, especially for start-up self-employeds. The chances of success are dramatically improving once the business starter has managed to get in charge of those issues.

Lack of goals

Goals, not goats. I didn't say anything about those always-hungry animals, of which there are plenty around where I live. So, those milk-producing goats are not the topic and will not be mentioned again in this book.

Instead, let's talk goals.

Lack of goals is common to almost all self-employed people, at least some of the time. This problem usually is tackled by the network organization with focus on two different incarnations: one approach for the longer-term goals, the other one for short-term goals.

Common to essentially all networks is the basic idea that a sponsor working with potential new partners should figure out their goals right at the beginning, oftentimes before they join. That's a good indication of the seriousness of your sponsor: if he doesn't care about your goals or whether you have any, the sponsor most likely doesn't care about you at all. Think twice before you are signing up with a mentor who doesn't care.

From the sponsor's perspective, it's important to understand where the new partner is standing right now and where he wants to go – if the noob is wishlessly happy, there is precious little the network can do for him. Any sponsor will ruin his teeth attempting to get somebody like that to actively engage in the business.

Unfortunately, many sponsors (at least in their own first months) do not recognize the importance of this goal-seeking session; that's as much true for their own goals as it is for the goals of the potential new partner. As a result, this part of the process ends up being cut short or – even worse – is dropped altogether. Which, in turn, causes severe damage to any chances for success.

And no, "making money" is not a goal. At least not a goal for which you would get over your dislike of picking up the phone and calling back 2 potential clients who sent you some emails asking for that call. Whom are you kidding?

Once you have signed up with a network organization, the company will continue to provide you with short-term goals – with the intention of getting you to at least aim at some short-term goals or milestones, rather than having none at all.

No doubt, externally imposed goals are by far less energizing and produce not nearly as much enthusiasm as your own self-chosen goals could do. However, at least I see the reason why the companies are trying to keep you from falling onto your coach and turning into a potato. As a coach potato, you usually don't sell much (bad for the network company) and commonly don't make much money (bad for yourself).

Just giving you a goal probably doesn't do much, so the network companies are throwing in some kind of reward – cash, trips to coveted destinations, cars...

A "coveted" destination is one which sounds great and where you usually wouldn't travel on your own. Therefore, the trophy rarely will be Columbus, Ohio. More often you will find Hawaii, Cancun or a Mediterranean cruise on the list of incentives.

Depending on the milestone you have reached in your quest for the goal, the company pays a smaller or larger share of the travel costs, usually up to the full trip costs for 2 persons.

Lack of strategy and/or written plan

Psychologists tell us what we should know anyway – at least on this topic. Any plans work much better if and when they are written down by the person who intends to execute them. Given this knowledge, any service provided by a network (or even the management in a non-network environment) can replace your own doing-it only to a very limited degree.

That said, networks commonly make standardized marketing plans available to you – and all of those marketing plans are aimed at you investing your personal time and labor. Which makes sense because you don't have much else to invest – otherwise you more likely would have purchased into a franchise, in which case you could employ lots of capital.

Traditional companies (or startups with a large line of credit with their bank) tend to just throw lots of money at advertising, believing that could solve their marketing job.

For you as a self-employed individual, that's frequently not much of an option because you don't have that much cash available – fortunately so. Instead, the networks suggest approaches to marketing which feature low capital costs, but in turn more personal time investment. Frequently, so-called home parties or sales parties are part of the mix, as well as inviting interest persons to participate in one of the regular network meetings or the – less regularly, but still frequent enough – network events (the events have a much bigger entertainment component).

Whether or not you personally like home parties, fact is that many networkers get most of their sales from just such parties. Further, most potential partners convert into signed-up partners only after participating in at least one major network event. Nevertheless, those instruments are not one-fits-all tools. There are ample of people outright repelled by the commonly loud and over-hyped network events (me, for one); also, participating in home parties for many people is unthinkable (me again). If you as networker are limiting your methods to such types of tools, you simply will not be able to reach a sizeable crowd of potential network marketing partners.

The obvious problem with many of the suggestions provided by network companies is: many, if not most network members don't work with and on the suggestions. Instead, they just try to memorize everything word for word and merely rattle off everything as soon as they can get hold of a warm body who doesn't instantly run away. The result is a rather wooden performance with a generous touch of mechanical boredom.

Put yourself in the shoes of a potential interested person: would you really like to attend such a questionable amateur play?

Postpone what you can get done today

Who did never encounter this one: you should be doing something actually important. But somehow, there is an internal force pushing you to postpone it anyway – despite the fact that usually there would be sufficient time to get it done right away.

Filing your tax return, paying bills, picking up the phone to call customers – does that ring a bell deep inside your head?

This issue is by far not limited to network marketing situations. Au contraire! The biggest problems with this habit do manifest in large-scale companies, for which sales by phone are a question of survival (insurances and publishing houses, to name but a few). Their sales people can't be bothered to actually call back customers who themselves have asked for a phone call. Not even under threat of dire consequences does anything change. Instead, many "tele-sales" workers are excessively creative to come up with "proof" why tele-marketing doesn't work anymore, why nobody picks up the phone, and why it's a bad week anyway.

Does that sound familiar? Well, large companies with deep pockets each spend hundreds of thousands every year paying for training to mitigate that problem – with at best mediocre outcomes.

Precisely the same danger threatens you as a work-from-home type of self-employed starter as well. We call it the "fridge-trap" – because for somebody working from home oftentimes the refrigerator (or its content, respectively) appears by far more important than calling customers or getting essential tasks done.

Network marketing companies try to counteract this force of gravity by centralizing tasks like invoicing, collecting money, shipping the products to the customer, sending current news and updates to your downline partners. They do all that stuff without networkers having to actively engage with it. The networkers also are paid their commissions without having to specifically request those payments.

Therefore, even if you as a partner in the network can't be bothered to contact your downline, at least the company tries to touch base with them regularly. Clearly, that's not a comprehensive solution – but it's by far better than no contact with your downline partners due to you falling into the fridge trap.

Now you just need to hand over your tax stuff to your CPA – and the most dangerous triggers for mental depression are off the table. What remains is the task to find and approach new customers and partners. Which is essentially the same problem all businesses have, regardless of their organization structure – it applies to airplane manufacturers just as well.

Price reduction as reason to buy

If you don't know your products by heart (i.e., their benefits and potential use cases) and you can't be bothered to learn about the specific personal situation and needs of your prospects, what remains as line of reasoning that could lead the customer to buy your product?

I don't know what you would say or do at this point – but I can tell you about the path followed by the overwhelming majority of startups (and a still large number of sales people with established companies). Namely, they cut the prices and hope this will sway the customer's bias towards the purchase.

Actually, decades-long experiences as well as comprehensive studies have shown clearly: price reductions in general do **not** lead to more profit or income. Especially not if the competition in the market is free to do precisely the same; that's called a price war. Very soon, nobody makes any money on the sale. At least at first, a price war seems to benefit the customer, but for the side of the seller, nobody benefits from that war. Just the same as with any other war.

For most part, network marketing companies have taken away any pricing power from their sales people. Networkers can't reduce the price and usually can't increase it, either. Giving rebates without gaining any additional value from the sale simply is not possible.

Sure, one can always find ways to get around the rules and abuse incentive offers to manipulate retail prices. But why? End users always have the option to buy into the marketing network and thereby get the option to purchase at wholesale prices in the future.

At first glance, the inflexible prices seem to be a substantial restriction: how can you market something if you can't adjust the prices?

However, I would argue it's a blessing in disguise. This restriction stops marketers from destroying prices and thereby set in motion the infamous price spiral of death (aka "race to the bottom"). Instead, the marketers have to compete by means of consultancy and analyzing customer needs.

Shouldn't the individual merchant retain authority to adjust prices as he sees fit? I agree; that makes sense. However, if you are a network marketer, you are in the business of marketing – not in the business of selling the product.

Let me explain:

If you were to work in an advertising agency, would you be able to change the price of a car at your own discretion just because it then would look better on the advertising billboard? Probably not, right?

How does signing-up usually work?

Normally, you enter such a network by paying the admission fee and purchasing a starter package. Supposedly, the starter package is the equivalent of your initial inventory stock (in case you would have opted for a traditional retail model.)

So far, there is nothing reprehensible.

The admission fee (or signup fee)

Networks charge a fee for merely signing you up. It comes under many different names and with different amounts – with the main point being that you don't receive any goods for the payment.

Oftentimes, there is some kind of reasoning provided for why that fee does provide a value, but that justification wouldn't be necessary – by contrast, franchise systems (which charge by far higher fees) drop the justification entirely and more or less tell you "If you want to get in, that's what you have to pay."

I suspect network companies are aware of most new sign-ups not being business people and therefore no professionals and consequently not familiar with the magnitudes of fees in other types of businesses. So, the network provides reasons which may or may not apply. Nowadays, most companies provide you with a shop web site for their products –that works as a justification for the fee.

What amounts are we talking? In most cases known to me, the entry fee runs between $1 and $100 as a one-off payment. Frequently, there is an ongoing annual fee, which is usually less than the initial fee.

Higher admission fees have become rare by now.

The starter package

You as a new member are expected and sometimes even required to buy a whole starter package. In many cases, you can choose from more than just one starter package; sometimes, there is only one.

In either case these starter packages should be a selection of products you can use to familiarize yourself with the products and, in case there is more than one of a kind of product in the package, to sell the other ones. If starter packages are laid out this way, they are a direct replacement for what a normal retailer would have to buy as well – whether or not it's called a package, doesn't matter much.

The pricing point for starter packages commonly is slightly below the sum of the products' individual prices.

What are warning signs?

1. If the wholesale(!) price sum of the individual products turns out to be less than the package price, that should raise some eyebrows
2. If starter packages are containing for most part stuff you are **not** allowed to sell to outsiders (=outside the network), that in my humble opinion would be a big warning sign. If, for example, the starter package contains merely training material, paper forms or anything else explicitly restricted to signed-up members – that forces you to first sign up new members before you can sell anything. In these cases, there is no market value that you could use to determine the real price-worthyness of the package. As such, it's worth-less

Whenever you sign up with a network marketing system and buy a starter package, the person signing you up (your mentor) is paid a commission. So far, that's legit and normal (the same is true if you buy a product anywhere else: the sales person will be paid from your purchase).

In the context of network marketing an important aspect would be whether the mentor's commission is derived from the package price or from the admission fee. The latter is a big no-no and in many countries outright illegal.

Why is that a problem? Does it really matter if the commission is tacked on top of the product price or on the admission fee?

In the eyes of the justice system, it does matter – and that, in turn, is all that matters for you and me. I assume you are reading this book because you don't want to be trapped in something a court will rule illegal soon after you joined, therefore we should step through the process of evaluating such packages.

Whenever you buy a bundled offer anywhere, clearly your alternative is to buy the contained items separately. Therefore, you should compare the sum of all individual item prices with the package price. I know, it's a no-brainer – but the operative part here is the "you." **You** should do the comparison – do never rely on somebody else's opinion. Surprisingly often, that somebody else never did the math but instead took his wisdom from yet another person who may or may not have been able to use the pocket calculator correctly.

Is the starter package more expensive than the sum of the components' wholesale prices? Big red flashing light! Somebody is trying to pick your pocket for additional money in order to pay for the sponsor's commission. In effect, that means the normal sale doesn't yield enough to pay for such commission – and this implies you are required to continuously find new members in order to make enough money for your own living simply because existing partners won't generate enough profits even if they buy reasonable amounts of product. That, esteemed reader, is the definition of a disguised chain letter scheme. Which is, of course, as illegal and dysfunctional as the undisguised chain letter.

Does the starter package have a lower price than the individual items? That's ok then – in this case, not only does the regular product sale produce sufficient gross profits to pay for the regular commissions but also allows for a small welcome discount for new partners.

Keep in mind: regardless of what your sponsor may be telling you – always use the wholesale prices for the products as the base for comparison, not the retail prices. Because: as soon as you have signed up, you can buy the products at wholesale prices. From this moment, retail prices don't matter for you anymore as a basis for comparison. That's why starter packages must not be more expensive than the sum of the wholesale prices for the products contained within the package.

Case study:

Your sponsor suggests a starter package due to the high discount you will be getting. This package consists of 3 skin care products:

1 facial cleanser

1 jar night cream

1 bottle day cream

The starter package altogether is priced at $180. The retail price is $260. Your sponsor is all excited about the fantastic rebate.

So – how great is that rebate, really? From the numbers you have been told so far, you cannot determine the real rebate. You sponsor conveniently forgot to tell you the wholesale prices, therefore you will explicitly ask for those!

If you get to know the wholesale discount normally runs at 35%, then you can go ahead and calculate: retail prices $260, minus 35% (=260*0.35, which is $91) leaves you with a wholesale value of the items of $169. But of course, you are getting the package at the wonderfully discounted price of – eh... $180 ?

In case you are living in a jurisdiction with a VAT regimen (value added tax or, Canada for example, GST = goods and services tax), the retail price will include this tax as well; the wholesale price, however, will not. That requires you to subtract that tax amount out of the retail price before you can compare anything. Let's assume your country imposes a 20% VAT; in this case, you reduce the retail price by 20%: $260 - $52, leaves $208 as the net retail price. Reduce this amount by the 35% wholesale discount mentioned above, and your package's value really is $135.20; but again, if you buy the package, you'll get it for the low price of $180. Can you spot the issue?

You are expected to pay 180 for a package you **know** you can buy tomorrow for only 135 (or 169, if in a non-VAT jurisdiction like the US).

How much commission will your sponsor receive for selling you this package? $10, $25 or something like that? Bad luck here – it is fairly obvious that this commission comes directly from your pocket, with no additional value provided to you. Sorry to say it, but again you are facing a chain letter system in disguise, to which some products have been added to blur the facts. If I were you, I would keep the hands off this thing!

To avoid a major misunderstanding: I don't have a shroud of a problem with salespeople getting a commission for their work. Sales people need to be paid just as anybody else does.

Neither do I have a problem with the manufacturer's expectation of you buying some of their products upon entering the network. After all, how could you advise anybody seriously on the products if you neither know them nor have any at hand to show and test?

I definitely do have some grievances when salespeople (or, in this case, sponsors) are paid a commission for something that demonstrably didn't provide any value. Your entering into the system isn't creating a value by itself. The system itself didn't provide any value either (remember: you could buy the very same products at a lower price). Whenever money is spread around without value being created simultaneously (or beforehand), then in effect your money is shuffled around – which happens to be the cornerstone of a rip-off.

I wouldn't go so far as to say it's fraud or theft, but I certainly have sympathies for anybody who would say so. That's a point where I am on the same line as law makers – laws and judges, too, want to see where and how commissions are actually earned and not just paid using somebody else's entry fee (regardless of how it's called).

Such methods are reserved for (government(!)-licensed) lotteries, where you simply pay money for the hope of receiving other people's money.

Is it a problem if the products' prices are just too expensive?

Not necessarily – "too expensive" is a very subjective term. And, sorry to say, your opinion doesn't count much in this context. If you can find customers who are willing to pay that price **without joining the network**, then apparently the product is **not** too high for everybody – and that suffices.

You don't want to sell to everybody on the planet but only to those for whom your product provides the necessary value. To use a well-known example from the car industry: not everybody can afford a Mercedes – but Mercedes nevertheless makes quite a living off its car sales. Nobody in his right mind would conclude this company to be a fraud or illegit.

The pricing on its own apparently can't be the deciding factor. The real question always is the value in the eyes of the customer – which most definitely is no question you could answer on behalf of potential customers. It's up to the consumer to make this decision; every customer is different and therefore has different values.

This aspect alone is enough reason for you to know your products and to know interested customers who can tell you how much they normally would pay for this product elsewhere. Having such people at hand can help to provide you with better insights into whether or not the product's price is competitive.

Either way, though, it has little to do with fraud. Companies produce literally boat loads of products every day, which in the end don't find anybody willing to buy them – that's the risk of every business.

Additional perks in the starter packages

More often than not, the network companies throw some additional benefits into those starter packages to attract you to higher-priced packages. That's fair, but it shouldn't keep you from first calculating the hard value of those packages – regardless of whether your sponsor insist on "anything less than the Premium Package doesn't make any sense".

Of course you would expect the sponsor to say just that, after all he derives his commission from the purchase price you are paying for that package. When your sponsor is claiming smaller packages don't make any sense, he is honestly telling the truth. From his point of view.

However, the truth from **your** point of view is your own responsibility. That's why it is your job to figure the hard value of the package (as shown in the previous subchapter). Leave out all additional perks and added stuff that you cannot sell or use as product. You will be operating a business, and unless something is making you money, it doesn't have a value.

Next, you can look at those perks you just left out of your calculation. Oftentimes, you are offered a better status rank for a limited time; we will talk about the meaning of those ranks later – for now, it mainly means you will get a slightly higher commission for the sales of your downline (we recall: downline is the team you have been building from new partners). The problem immediately surfacing is: how large is your downline right now?

Right... there is nobody. You are just starting yourself. How much commission do you get from that non-existent downline? Also none, of course.

Now let's say the purchase of the more expensive starter package gives you an added bonus of 10% on all downline commissions for the next 60 days. What might be your monetary benefit from that? Hmm... 10 percent of nothing. That would be – still nothing.

Essentially, this added bonus for you is kind of worthless unless you have a ton of people signing up together with you (which happens!) If this added bonus is the only perk in the package, you are paying a lot of money for a status rank pin which may look a bit nicer. If that's what you're aiming at, go for it...

Otherwise, feel free to ignore these sweeteners and directly compare the package prices to the product prices (always use the wholesale prices for comparisons!)

If you now notice that the higher-priced packages offer a better rebate (as a percentage), then indeed you may consider whether you can use those additional products in your marketing efforts.

However, if there is no additional rebate to be had – or, worse, the rebate is shrinking as the prices rise – then you should question whether you really want to continue in this system. Here's why:

If you have figured out that it's better to buy a cheaper package, how likely is it that your potential partners will figure it out, too? I'd say it should be highly likely because, as an honest mentor, you will tell them. And do so before they find it out on their own.

Once your potential partners have noticed this fact, you will end up selling at best several small packages, which unnecessarily limits the value of your time. It takes about the same time to sell a small package as it takes to sell a large one. If your company's pricing rewards buying small, that cuts into your commission for no apparent reason.

What you want to see is the opposite: the pricier the package (and consequently the higher your commission), the higher should be the rebate the buyer gets. That way, you can recommend the higher-priced packages with a clean conscience. Your new partner – if he can afford the big package – can save some money as a result of your recommendation.

To wrap it up: you can feel good about recommending the big-ticket package, your partner saves a pretty penny, **and** you are paid a higher commission for this sale. That is how it should work. Anything else is economically questionable.

When you are just starting your business, you don't need to make things more complicated than necessary. Means: if this network company didn't figure out the pricing of the starter packages by now, chances are they haven't figured out a lot of other stuff, either. Skip it and look for somebody who knows what they are doing.

Autoships and subscriptions

Most networks expect from you regular monthly orders. If you're just starting out, that certainly can feel like a millstone around your neck – repeatedly ordering stuff you don't need, that mainly implies expenses draining your already scarce cash.

Even more reason to carefully look at those subscriptions or autoships (the exact naming differs).

Is the monthly order mandatory?

Does it have to be a subscription for the same product, or can you make month-by-month choices?

If it has to be a subscription for the same product over and over, that might turn out to be a problem – in this case, write down a minus-sign somewhere on your evaluation sheet.

Can you omit this monthly order if you can live with the penalty?

Some networks penalize you for not meeting your monthly minimum purchase by not paying you commissions for your partners' sales, but you will get commissions for your own sales either way. In such cases, you probably can live without paying for the monthly minimum order. As long as you don't have a downline, it doesn't hurt to lose their commissions, right? This way, you can very well start building your retail business without having to deal with the minimum order albatross.

Do retail orders placed by your customers count towards your minimum order?

That would be great – in this case, your network just requires you to do just something at all, if you want to remain partner; they wouldn't care whether your customer ordered directly or you ordered for your own account. This version of the rule shouldn't cause any headaches because, if you neither have customers nor are buying anything for yourself – what are you doing in this business? This situation would be reason to reconsider your business idea. If the monthly minimum order turns out to be the pressure point nudging you towards thinking, even better.

Remains the question: how much is the required minimum amount?

Most networks fall somewhere below $200; if you reflexively react to this number with a statement like "that stuff ends up in my garage and just costs me money", then indeed you have a problem – the problem of thinking like a retail customer.

Picture a different approach. Instead of joining a network marketing organization, you have set up a retail store. Your wholesaler requires you to purchase monthly at least for the same amount that the network requires, say $200 – just to keep your retailer account alive. Most likely, you would give the wholesaler a friendly smile and respond "sure, no problem." Such a purchase volume per month is not too high but too low by far. If this minimum poses a problem for your business, then you have another, much larger issue: you are lacking customers.

Absence of customers can and will kill any business. If the monthly minimum order value is what brings that to your attention, then that's a good thing. It easily could save you from several years of agonizing pain.

If the amount of the minimum order represents a problem for you, then there is not much left for you to do – you are simply lacking the basic necessities for self-employment. Go get a job. Really, I'm serious.

You can come back at a later time and re-evaluate the whole thing, but if right now that relatively low amount is a serious issue for you, make sure to stabilize your finances before you venture into a business risk. Otherwise, the smallest dent in your sales might lead you to decisions, which you will regret dearly in not too distant future.

A problem of a different kind can be caused by the minimum monthly order if all those circumstances come together:

- You are not part of your own target group and therefore do not use the products yourself (that happens; not every lawnmower salesperson happens to own a garden)
- Customer orders do **not** count towards your monthly minimum; regardless of how many sales you are referring, you still have to buy for yourself (that obviously depends on your network)
- Your customers are not in your region; for example, you're living in Ohio, but your customers are in Mexico

The combination of these circumstances represents a problem – you have to order for delivery to your own address, but neither can you sell the merchandise to your customers nor do you have any use for the products yourself.

If such a situation is shaping up and the network company doesn't want to adjust their policy, then this network isn't suitable for you – plain and simple.

Under no circumstance should you settle for a helpful suggestion from your sponsor, according to which you order your minimum required shipment and your sponsor then will buy it from you because she surely has use for the products. That might be true - as long as the sponsor is living in your area and still is part of the same network.

People change, their plans change – and your hypothetical sponsor wouldn't be the first one hopping from network to network, always on the quest for the pot of gold at the end of the rainbow. Unfortunately, so she figures out, there is no need for skin lotion once she has moved on and now sells vacuum cleaners. In which case she will not consider herself bound to the original agreement. Surely, you will understand?

Status ranks

If networks are really good at one thing, it must be creative invention of status ranks. Whether named after gemstones (Jade, Ruby, Sapphire, Diamond...), precious metals (Bronze, Silver, Gold, Palladium...), or something like military ranks, it doesn't matter: the network marketing organizations are full of them.

Those ranks are designed to give members the feeling of having climbed up the corporate ladder – because that's precisely what they can't do: climb a corporate ladder in a network of self-employeds. You're all independent, you don't have a boss, and you aren't the boss of anybody. Everybody is responsible for his or her own income as a result of the sales success – which does or does not materialize every month anew.

Early on, the networks couldn't help but notice that, for many self-employed persons, it seems to be a problem to not be able to climb up the corporate ladder.

This apparently is not so much a financial problem as it is a mental issue: we humans have come to crave the experience of being promoted within a hierarchy. Even if the bank account clearly states how successful we are, we still seem to need an additional validation by others – preferably in a way everybody will recognize. That's the purpose of stripes and pins in military hierarchies.

Other organizations have other status symbols. Point in case, I have worked with a company, which emphasized the status of a person by regulating the number of plants that person had to have in the office. If you wanted to estimate the importance of a person, count that person's office plants. (I am really talking about that leafy green stuff which needs to be watered regularly)

In other companies, the symbol is location and/or size of the offices ("C-level floor"). And so on.

None of those applies to a sales person working from home, the office frequently being the kitchen table. I myself am working at home from a desk in my lounge. That won't change, regardless how successful I am – or not.

Now, how does one create public recognition and announce a rise in a hierarchy when there actually is no hierarchy?

Networks have solved this problem by attaching status ranks to certain performance thresholds. On network events, recent rank promotions are then publicly recognized – by inviting all new Ruby-members on stage, by presenting them with status rank pins, or even by asking them to hold a brief speech.

Whether you personally think this to be important doesn't matter – your future partners might have a very different take on that. We humans are different, and networks are trying to provide incentives for at least the majority of people types.

If you are looking at a network that doesn't provide such incentives – ask yourself hard and repeatedly if you can live with that. If a network doesn't offer such status ranks, at some time you will run into problems with team partners who need just that type of recognition. In those cases, either **you** have to provide it – or you will quickly loose them again. That would be a pity because, the more different you and your partners are, the more successful your team can address different customer groups.

What does a status rank do?

Now that you know the reason for the existence of status ranks, we have to discuss what they are good for (besides providing pins or stickers).

Rank improvements are usually triggered by a combination of team size and purchase volume generated by your team – hardly a surprise, those numbers being the key performance indicators for the network company itself.

Your team consists of all the new partners you have enrolled with the network and which therefore have been placed "under you" on the org chart of the network. That's your so-called downline, and those are the very same partners for whose sales you are receiving commissions.

Team revenue consists of all orders your partners have either placed themselves or which have been transacted through their retail accounts. Most networks don't make a difference between own purchases and retail purchases.

Once you passed certain thresholds, you will be "promoted." Those promotions in the beginning usually come quite quickly. Often having only two partners is sufficient to promote you for the first time.

Thereafter, depending on the network, the next promotion happens with 4 to 8 partners, next when reaching 12 to 16 partners, after that it gets a bit more difficult – after all, there are network teams with several thousand partners. If you would be promoted every time the next 4 partners sign up, the network very soon would run out of available gemstone or precious metal names for the ranks.

Each new rank usually gives you a slight improvement in terms of your compensation – mostly regarding the commission you are receiving for the activities of your team partners.

That all sounds fairly theoretical – an unfortunate side effect of anything finance. To figure out what it means for the network in question and for your personal situation, I suggest you ask your inviting sponsor to do some math for you while you are sitting with him anyway.

Think about how much you need to live on, and then ask him which status rank you would need to have in order to make that kind of money. It helps to add the question how much sales volume you or your team would need to reach for that to become reality.

To be clear: the answer to this question in no case will be a promise or guarantee – we keep in mind, the sponsor is neither able nor legally allowed to make such promises! If the sponsors does it anyway, you should quickly come up with an excuse and leave the premises – or kick him off yours.

You may phrase your inquiry something like this:

"I would like to get an idea of what's required to make this thing work. If, sometime down the road, I need $3000 per month before taxes in income to live on – which status rank would one need to have for that kind of income in your network, and from which types of compensation would those commissions be derived?"

Assuming you didn't ask for an absurd amount (here: $3000, which would be a normal amount to ask for), your sponsor should be able to give you an answer right away. If he can't do that, that simply means he did not reach this point himself. That's ok, but in this case he should bring somebody to the table who is able to answer this question from own experience.

If he can't bring anybody who does know, chances are that nobody did get there. I find it hard to believe that you of all people would be the first one to reach any specific income level in the organization – more likely, this could be a huge warning sign!

However, an answer you should expect would be something like "To make that kind of income, you commonly would be a Ruby member. In this case, you would have to have 200 commission cycles per month; from those cycles would come $5000. Whatever you yourself generate in direct retail sales, yields 30% and goes on top of that amount, but your own retail sales often fluctuate much more than your team commissions."

In this case, he at least has a good working knowledge how a sales-person with a basic income would look like. But please, those are not stars of the marketing world – they are able to live off it, not much more.

If you are living outside the United States and are quoted the amounts in US$ anyway, that should not be of concern; networks are usually international in nature, and international finance transactions are most commonly based on the US$. The commission amounts would be converted to your local currency upon transfer to your bank account.

I hope you noticed the answer contained a term, which is undefined so far ("cycles") – in such cases, you **must** ask for the meaning of this term. Frequently, networks have their own internal transaction units (precisely because of their international nature) and you should understand what this transaction unit is worth. Unifying sales to a currency-independent unit (be it US$ or be it some artificial number) makes sense, but you definitely need to know what it is.

Whenever a certain number of transaction units has been reached, you receive a credit for one commission unit. Not every organization calculates this way, but this method seems to spread; other companies continue to base their calculations on one of the major currencies (US$ or Euro, for example) and come up with a simple commission amount – but in this case, they tend to have some stipulation that says commissions of less than, say, $50 are not paid out. That's because networks try to protect themselves against the need to transfer half a million tiny payments of a few cents each. Banks don't work for free, and if the banking fees exceed the commission value, somebody will have a problem.

Either way, you should expect some kind of minimum payout requirement, which can be stated outright ("must be at least $50") or the commission units are granted only in full numbers (and then one commission unit might be worth about $50).

Regardless – you should know how much the minimum required payout happens to be. If you find it to be oddly high, such as $500 or so, then you should probably distance yourself from this network. Would you be able to keep your enthusiasm if you don't see any money for the first few months? I doubt it.

Now that you know you need to be Ruby member, your next question should be:

"To reach Ruby status – what are the requirements for that?"

The answer might be something like "You will need 12 personally sponsored Amethyst partners in your team, and you need to reach 200 cycles per month."

So, you need to have 200 cycles – which explains why he previously said, Ruby members have 200 cycles: that's the requirement because otherwise you aren't a Ruby member. Simple.

And you need at least 12 Partners who did sign up with you directly (not indirectly with somebody else in your team) and therefore are in your downline – of which at least 12 need to have Amethyst status rank.

You could go on and inquire about the prerequisites for Amethyst status, since you need to help your team partners to get to that status rank (otherwise you'll flunk the Ruby).

If you aren't especially good at sketching such diagrams in your head, ask your sponsor to draw up your required team. Once you see it on paper, you know where you need to get.

Next, you should ask how much sales is needed to achieve those 200 cycles.

The result should fall somewhere between $200K and $300K ("K" = thousands). If the number were much lower than that, the implication would be you are receiving substantially more than 1% of your team's sales as commission. In this case, ask how that is possible – the company cannot pay out more commission than it took in as payment. If all other partners have already taken their cut, you get yours, and your up-line (the sponsor in front of you and his sponsor) wants a commission also, then this doesn't leave much for the manufacturer. That's why much larger percentages are usually unsustainable in the long term.

I will admit, higher percentages are possible if there is a plausible limitation built-in. For example, if commissions are only paid for the first 4 levels of your downline, that explains the higher percentages because your sources of commissions are much fewer. In this case, however, you probably should go back and have your sponsor show how your $3000 monthly income is supposed to be generated.

Oh – and make sure to explicitly ask for the sales volume expressed in retail prices. That's quite a chunk more than stating it in wholesale prices. Since you need to know how much your team needs to **sell** (not buy), you need to know the retail value.

Did you, by chance, just fall off your chair when reading the amount 200K to 300K?

Welcome to reality, my friend! If you are a retailer, 300K sales revenue is an amount you should be shooting for if you expect to pay for costs and purchase prices, and still have something left over for yourself.

Since the sponsor's response was specifically referring to the commissions you receive for your team's sales (and not for sales you personally closed with retail customers), that amount can be directly compared to the amounts you would see when operating a traditional store with employees, where only employees are doing the selling. In that case, you would have to pay their salaries, payroll taxes and associated costs, and ultimately you most likely would end in a similar magnitude as the $3000.

Please note – that is only your compensation as business owner. It does **not** include your "salary" as salesperson (the gross profit when you are selling directly to retail customers). However, this salary-like component at least in the beginning will be a substantial part of your commission.

Since you cannot slice yourself up into several parts and thereby get more sales with more customers, there is a natural soft upper limit to how much you can earn by doing the selling yourself.

Every business owner is aware of that – that's why many have employees. In network marketing, you don't have employees – that's what your partners are for.

As time progresses and your business hopefully continues to improve, your retail commission will drop (as a percentage of your total income) and your team commission will rise. That's intended and necessary. If you continue to solely rely on your retail sales, then ask what will happen in case an illness gets hold of you.

Your personal sales drop, the retail commission drops as well, and your income is gone. Not a pretty picture. Wouldn't be as painful if a major part of your commission came from your team's sales.

After we have determined the downline to be an important long-term source of income for you, we now will hit a major road block, unexpected by most starters.

Break-Away

Neither does break-away sound good nor is it good. Enough reason to talk about it.

We have seen how your status depends on the number of and the sales from partners who have signed up with you.

We also have seen that your team commission comes from the sales of those very partners. Essentially, every partner means real hard cash for you.

You can print your exit ticket from the daily rat race as employee or self-employed by building a sales team, from which you then will derive a small commission for each sale for the rest of your and their membership lives. It's your responsibility to accumulate enough small trickles to make up a large stream.

Good idea.

Once this commission stream is swelling over time, you can lean back and relax a bit more often – may it be 6 or 10 years in the future. The 2 years frequently mentioned by your sponsor, those you should forget about. They are as realistic as unicorns and tooth fairies.

But let's not argue about the time spans, it's about the principle: at some time, you will reach the point when you get rewarded for all the work, when you can harvest the fruits of your past labor. Right?

That's the plan, yes.

Unfortunately, several networks have some fine print likely to screw up your plans faster than you may expect: Break-Away.

After you have won a sizeable number of sales partners, you will notice that there are tons of people who simply do nothing. Nothing at all. Not only do they not do anything, they don't even **want** to do anything for their business.

Those partners, you should simply forget about. That's a quirk of life and the universe – just as there are tons of workers in any major company who seem to get paid for just showing up. Fortunately, in network marketing you don't have to pay for them.

Then, a second group consists of people who achieve some sales and therefore contribute to your income – but they themselves can't live off their commissions. That's a pity, but for most part it's the result of their own choices.

Last, but not least, there are those extremely few who treat network marketing as a real business, a commercial endeavor, and who act accordingly. Means: a shop owner cannot afford to simply close the shop for the day because he doesn't feel like being bothered by customers (I said: **cannot afford**. I know quite well that there are ample self-employed people who **are doing** just that. Alas, those are exactly the ones closing their shop soon thereafter for good).

Who has been hustling from dawn til dusk in his network marketing business, will almost inevitably be successful eventually. Provided he's working with a reputable network company.

Such sales partners you want to have in your downline, of course. You wouldn't be bothered if such people have more sales partners than you do. As long as you get the commission, everything is good. Right?

Well – and that's where the fertilizer hits the fan. Some networks have a mechanism baked into their rules, which will be triggered once the status rank (i.e. the success) of your downline partner exceeds your own status rank. In this case, this super-partner breaks away from your downline and will be attached somewhere above you – saving the network company a lot of money (**your commission**) and robbing your income.

This super-partner and usually all of his downline is gone from your commission check. The main source of your income is gone – forever. You have worked years to get there, just to see the network taking away your success.

That, for me, is an absolute no-go. If a system is designed to emphasize the postponed income type as much as network marketing is by definition, then they can't pull the carrot away after you reached it. "Can't" is to be meant liberally – it's obvious they can. It's just wrong, in my opinion.

If you encounter such a system, you need to ask yourself: do I want to enter into a business to make money, or do I just want to buy their products at a discount? If it's only for the discount on your personal consumption – ok, in that case you can go ahead and sign up (provided, no other obstacle is hiding in their contracts).

You wanted to build your business fortune on this network? Forget it. You would be building a house on quicksand. You must be able to rely on commissions coming for as long as your team makes sales – regardless, whether you are suffering MS or cancer in a hospital room or you are climbing the Himalayas in pursuit of a life-long dream of yours.

A network with break-away mechanism is deadly for your plans.

How are you going to earn?

Very likely one of the most boring parts of the network marketing presentation is the compensation plan (probably clocking in on second rank right after compliance requirements, which for precisely that reason are frequently omitted from any presentation anyway).

However, the compensation plan also is the most important part. It's nothing less than the collection of rules how and for what you will be paid. This is something you really need to understand. If you don't – don't complain about being ripped off afterwards.

Compensation plans commonly have two essential components and several others that you could view as the icing on the cake. Those cake-icing-components are widely different between the networks – but since they don't contribute much to your income at least for the first several years, we will reduce them to a few sentences later. For now, bread and butter are more important for you, I would expect.

Retail commission

Whenever you are referring a retail sale, in most networks you have earned a retail commission. Some networks are differentiating between sales to real end users and sales to new partners just signing up; the basic idea is the same: you refer a sale and receive a commission for doing so. "Referring a sale" means: a customer, using your retail account, is buying from the network company. These days, that's often accomplished by buying from the web site the company gave you to send your customers to.

Alternatively, you can sell merchandise to a customer by yourself and take the product from your own stock of products. In this case, you purchased the merchandise at wholesale prices and you sold it at retail prices. While the difference now is called the profit margin, for all intents and purposes it's similar to the retail commission you would have received when referring the sale directly to the network company.

Most networks even treat the two cases identical as long as the customers are regular retail customers.

However, if the network offers special discounts for frequent customers, then the calculation will look different – in those cases, it's required for the customers to order directly from the network company (using your account) in order to obtain those special discounts.

The only important aspect for you remains: if the customers need to order directly from the company, that of course means you cannot use those customers to sell your inventory. Keep that in mind when stocking up on products.

Question at the core obviously would be: how much retail commission do you receive, and which products are you selling? Are those consumption items or are you dealing with machines or appliances? Appliances and machines have a much longer product life and consequently will be purchased far less often than consumption items. That should be reflected in your commissions.

Although – selling appliances and machines often is just the "foot in the door" for selling specific consumption items. The "real" business model is selling consumption items, not the appliance. As any user of an inkjet printer should be able to witness: printer was almost free, the ink certainly isn't.

Does the richness of your retail commission almost match the thickness of a razor blade, i.e. is below 10%? Then, please, let your sponsor do the math for you how anybody is supposed to earn anything off this product. May well be this network has found a solution for that issue – I haven't encountered a company with such slim margins and still able to generate even a remote chance for their sales teams.

Lower limit of acceptable commission usually is about 25%, a decent percentage starts at 30%. However, if this number exceeds 50% you should be wary of the products just being too expensive. Before you sign up with this sponsor, ask potential buyers for the products how much they are paying for similar products elsewhere. Get an idea of the market prices for your (future) competition. And please: competition does not refer to just another network marketing company. Every consumer always has the option to pay a visit to the corner store next street and see if the product is available there!

Team commissions

If you are bringing new partners into the network organization, you are building an own team – that much you probably figured by now. You are mentoring this team, and in turn you are paid a team commission. This commission goes by many names, but there isn't much of a difference – it always amounts to getting a small commission for the sales of your partners.

Again – a Warning!

If you are receiving a commission just for signing up a new partner, without that partner having purchased anything that could be the source of any value creation – then feel free to assume you have a problem, usually at least one of the legal type. These cases with high probability are not network marketing systems (where was the marketed product, implied by the term "marketing"?) but instead you are part of an illegal chain letter scam. As I have pointed out before, the courts see it this way: if you participate, you go to prison.

Limiting commissions

All partners enrolled by you (and under you) represent your first partner level (or first downline level, depending on how you want to call that).

Once those level-1-partners sign up new partners on their own, the new partners in turn become **their** level-1-partners. For you, however, they are only indirect partners, which we consequently call level-2-partners.

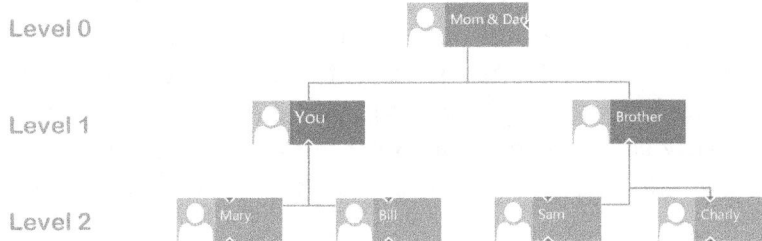

The same continues with additional partners signing up under those level-2-partners, which makes those newcomers (from your point of view) level-3-partners. And so on – nothing new under the sun.

Hypothetically, this way about 7 billion levels could be formed – if every inhabitant of planet Earth would sign up under another one.

That's highly unlikely, but that doesn't matter for the point I am try-ing to get at. Important is: in theory, this almost infinite depth could happen.

How does the network deal with the situation of exorbitant numbers of levels coming into existence? If there would be almost unlimited many levels, and all levels were to receive a commission on a sale, the commissions would explode into unlimited heights. Whoever believes in unlimited commissions on a limited planet like Earth is either a mad man or an economist. Often both.

Fact is, if you are promised 1% commission for a sale on each level, then a simple sale 80 levels below you will turn out to be dangerous for the company; not just you will expect to receive 1% commission, but also all other 79 levels below you are expecting the same type of commission payments. 80 levels with 1% each makes for an 80% com-mission off that one sale. If now the direct seller receives a retail com-mission (as she should!), then there is nothing left for the network company to pay for production and raw materials.

It should be fairly obvious that something has to give.

This is the reason why every network must have built-in some kind of limit to make sure the commissions do not grow sky-high.

Basically, there are 3 different approaches available: limiting the number of levels for which a commission is paid, limiting the commis-sion percentages for different levels, and limiting the time.

Limiting the number of levels

Quite often the networks do impose a limit for how many levels you will be paid a commission. In many cases the end is reached some-where between level 6 and level 10 – which means for you that you will not receive any commissions for anything happening more than level 10 below you (or wherever the specific level limit is placed).

This limitation is easy to comprehend while unfortunately also im-posing a problem: if your levels 1 and 2 are numb nuts doing nothing, your income will be derived only from level 3 onwards; should you have your cut-off level sitting at 5, that won't leave much opportunity for the multiplying power of networks to unfold their many-folding features.

Frequently you will receive commissions for more levels as your own status rank rises – which usually means you are starting with very few levels contributing to you commission check.

Limitation by means of reducing commission percentages

Another variant consists of limiting the percentages you will be paid from each level as commission. For example, the first level might yield 10%, the second level only 5%, the 3rd level only 2% and so on up to level 5 or so, when the percentage drops to insignificant. If your commission percentage for level 15 is 0.000001%, then it doesn't matter much whether you have 5000 partners on that level – simple math shows why: 5000 partners x 0.000001% = 0.005%; assume those 5000 partners all sell goods worth $100 per month, that's 500K per month, of which you will receive 0.005%. So, your commission check will amount to 500K * 0.005% = $25 per month. Sure, it's not literally nothing – but for a network of 5000 partners, it's very close to zilch.

For practical purposes, the system of percentage reduction imposes a similar limit to the system of limiting levels. It's just a different method of calculating the limit.

Limiting the time

This type of limit puts a lid on commissions, based on time. The most commonly found versions are:

Limitation of time the commission is paid

This simply means you will receive downline commissions for only the first 6 or 12 months or so, thereafter your downline will not contribute to your income any longer. That's not much different from your downline disappearing altogether.

Therefore, this system looks very much like a time-controlled automatic break-away; as you may recall, I consider the break-away idea insulting to begin with, so an automatic time-controlled break-away is no better.

Really, if you are willing to go with time-controlled break-away, you may as well just keep your 9-to-5-job and continue running in your personal rat race – with time-controlled break-away, you have to always run faster than your past success is breaking away from you due to the calendar. Bad idea, in my book.

Cap on the commission amount per time unit

In systems with this type of limitation, your commission claims are summed up, but you only receive the payments up to a fixed maximum amount per time unit. I happen to know a network that imposes such a restriction on a weekly base: in any given week, your team commission cannot exceed the limit of $26250. This way, your monthly income from team commissions is capped at about $105000.

This type of time limitation is by far more compatible with your intention of building a base income stream by building up your team partner structure; an amount of up to $100K helps to get through soft patches even if you can't close any retail sales yourself, I would think.

As long as your team commission is less than the weekly $26250 limit, this cap doesn't affect you at all – which is great especially for starters, who hardly will run into an issue with this cap. At the same time, caps like this ensure the viability of the network as a whole.

Incentive commissions

Your downline commissions tend to be slim or lacking altogether – especially over the first several months of your network marketing career, should you decide to pursue one. People, which we happen to be for better or worse, are quite quick in jumping ship reasoning, "it will never amount to anything." Jumping ship, of course, is not in the interest of the network company. They need you to sell their products and services.

The usual method to counteract the problem of early departure consists of additional incentives provided to sales partners who don't have much of a downline yet. Once you have a decent downline, nobody needs to tell you how great the system works – you can see it. Or you can't, in which case something might be wrong with the system or yourself.

As long as there is no downline, there also is no downline commission. The network companies try to make up for that perceived "shortfall" by offering bonuses for making reasonable steps towards building your sales team.

A good part of those bonuses consists of plain hard cash – which is exactly what a starting network marketing partner needs most. No, the network companies aren't stupid – the longer you stay, the likelier it gets that you will be successful. If you are making money, they make even more. That's how it works.

Those incentive offers, called promotions (short: promos), tend to run for only short periods of time – just enough to get your behind off the couch and call back a few prospects. Common time frames are 3 weeks to 2 months.

The incentive payments can run anywhere between a few hundred and several thousand dollar – amounts that won't make you a millionaire, but which can be extremely helpful to get off the ground and keep going even if you don't see much financial result otherwise.

If you make a decision for a specific network, do **not** (I repeat: NOT) include those incentive payments in your economic calculation and decision for or against this network!

For one, it is entirely unclear if such promotions will be offered after you have signed up (incentive promotions are completely voluntary on part of the network company). The other aspect is: you have no clue if you will be able to earn any of those incentive payments. Therefore leave them out of your decision process!

But: Once you have signed up and are looking for income, incentives become an important source of stress-relieve. You would be outright negligent to ignore those offers and leave that money on the table.

How you can make use of the respective current incentives and how you can plan to reach the goals, that depends a good deal on the network in question and the promotion offered at that time. This definitely is a case you should discuss and plan together with your mentor; you need to understand the details of the promotion's fine print – and make the most out of it.

That said, let me point one thing out, which seems to hold true in general: incentive promotions tend to focus on you improving your status rank and additionally hitting certain sales targets. Therefore, it's generally a good idea to first focus on the sales – and plan building up your status rank slowly and diligently. A case study highlights the reasons:

Assume the lowest status rank in your network is named BLUE. The next higher rank is GREEN, then YELLOW, and above that there comes RED. Your current status rank is BLUE (the lowest).

Now, such the January promotion comes along:

Runs: 4 weeks.

Rise to GREEN and generate at least $2000 wholesale volume; bonus $200

Rise to YELLOW and generate at least $4000 wholesale volume; bonus $500

Rise to RED and generate at least $8000 wholesale volume; bonus $1000

Short and sweet. But it's a heavy hitter.

How likely is to achieve $8000 sales volume (at wholesale prices!) in the next 4 weeks, if you haven't even reached the lowest level so far? Probably not all that likely, right?

Let's play with the thought you're able to achieve status rank RED, but your team manages only $3000 in sales. What bonus will you receive?

Probably the $200 bonus because you qualified for neither the $500 nor the $1000 bonus – but you did manage more than $2000 sales and you surpassed GREEN, so the $200 it is.

Now, let's assume just two months later the March promotion stops by with exactly the same terms. How much bonus can you get this time? Sobering answer: nothing.

That's because you **are** already RED at the start of the promotion, so you cannot "rise to RED" anymore. No matter how much in sales you can produce – there will be no bonus payment for you.

Therefore, first make sure you have the required revenue safely tucked away before attempting the status rank climb. In our case study you could first make sure you get to the $2000 sales in the January promo before you sign up your last partner(s) to advance to GREEN status. With that, you have pocketed the $200 bonus. **Then**, you continue working on reaching the next sales target. In our example, that failed (you ended at $3000 revenue), so you received $200 bonus – so far, there is no difference to the previous outcome except your status now is only GREEN, not RED. Sounds disappointing? It isn't.

Now the March promotion offers the same bonus amounts on same terms – but this time, you **can** participate. Your current status is only GREEN, so you still may advance to YELLOW or RED.

Again, your focus should be on sales first. Status is only a second thought. If (and only if) you reach the $4000 sales target, then you can try to quickly wrap up the deal by signing up waiting partners (which maybe you could have pushed a bit more to sign up earlier, but as you see: that wouldn't benefit you. Nor them).

Should you fall short and not manage the jump to YELLOW, you don't get a bonus this time. Next time around, you can give it a shot again.

Should the step to YELLOW work out, you will get the $500 bonus in the March promotion.

If this promotion comes back in the future, you can use the exactly same method to shoot for the $8000 sales target **and then** advance to RED status. If it works out, you'll receive the $1000 bonus. If it doesn't, you can try it with the next promotion thereafter.

My proposed way of dealing with those promotions not only is more profitable on the bottom line (you'll receive 3 bonus payments for a total of $1700 instead of otherwise just the maximum $1000) but even a failure to hit the target is not the dead end. You can try again until you make it. In other words: this version is substantially safer.

Insight: Rip-Off or Messianic Gift?

We're now through your maybe first in-depth confrontation with network marketing systems. What can you take home from our discussion?

Is network marketing really the savior of the new century, the divine gift many sponsors make it out to be?

Hardly. Network marketing is, and here the terminology is surprisingly honest, first and foremost a type of marketing. It is a form of self-employed entrepreneurship.

If you don't want to have anything to do with sales or marketing, most likely network marketing will not be a place where you will find your happiness.

However, you need to be aware: even traditional business models are spending commonly more than half of their revenue on some kind of marketing and sales promotion. In other words, most money from any sale anywhere goes to the people who do the marketing and the sales. Not manufacturers get the large cut, not the logistics companies, and certainly not the traditional retailers.

It's the marketing people who are draining the biggest bucks from everybody else – simply because they provide the most difficult service: get the customer's attention.

If you decide you don't want to be involved with sales or marketing, you are doing two things: you push away the biggest pot of gold in your vicinity. And you are putting yourself at the mercy of those who do the marketing. Self-employed persons are for most part in the business of marketing – regardless what they (and you) believe which business they are in.

Is network marketing the rip-off that all of your relatives and friends believe it to be?

I hope I was able to show in this book: yes, there are more than enough attempted assaults on your money, which dress up as network marketing systems.

But fraud is fraud, no matter how they call themselves. Enron was no network marketing company, the same holds true for MCI Worldcom.

Both corporate collapses due to fraud and illegalities have been spectacularly bombastic. You don't need to be a network marketing company to commit fraud. Nor are you looking at fraud whenever you are looking at a network marketing business.

However:

Network marketing is a very special case because, for most part, it is addressing people who have not been merchants (or otherwise self-employed) beforehand. Actually, most people had no intention of getting into self-employment before the initial conversation with a network sponsor.

This set of circumstances makes things problematic because the sponsor in those cases has a special obligation for disclosing and advising; even though the laws currently do not expose sponsors to fiduciary obligations, ethically it's not far away from that: if a sponsor is inviting a new partner into the network, he **must** be aware that, for the time being, he (the sponsor) is the only common ground the newbie happens to have with the world of self-employment.

Sure, everybody is his or her own boss and everybody is responsible for one self. Nevertheless, since all sponsors are fully aware of the situation, I believe they have an ethical obligation to serve as mentor in the real meaning of this word. Not just on paper.

Precisely that's where we see huge deficits, in my experience. Not just do sponsors neither want to afford time and motivation to take on that job. No, they themselves more often than not have simply no clue. Even worse, they don't want to have any clue. Somehow it feels as if they believe "If I don't know what I'm doing, it's less bad."

It isn't. It's worse. And that's what puts network marketing so close to fraud.

If somebody from within my own organization, some levels above me and featuring an impressive sounding status rank, approaches me with the offer to sign up with his brand-new Bitcoin-MLM – then I really do scratch my head and am wondering: this guy just managed to violated all rules there were to violate. Nevertheless, he expects me to ride into battle at his side?

Almost all network marketing contracts stipulate: you are not allowed to recruit from your downline for other networks. That's true for the network he and I are members of, too.

⇨ This rule he definitely violated

In pretty much every network contract (ours, for example) it clearly states you are **not** allowed to participate in any other network at the same time.

⇨ He violated that one, too

I have mentioned all the laws and legal regulations in the context of Bitcoin when I was talking about chain letter scams. He violated all of them.

Finally, he's getting snotty when I declined in a friendly manner, but pointing to the legal situation.

Sorry – those guys are the precise reason for network marketing having such a bad rap. And yes, my first contact with MLMs decades ago was exactly somebody like that.

But then, just because a car manufacturer has been lying his socks off with respect to fuel efficiency and emissions, that's no reason for giving up car travel. There may be different reasons to do so, but a lying manufacturer is none of them.

Accordingly, bad apples in network marketing are no reason to cross this business model off the list, either. They are a reason to look very closely at the claims made, though.

As self-employed person, you always will be learning on the job, while you are working. It can be very valuable to have somebody to talk to who does the same as you do – it helps tremendously with the exchange of experiences and lessons learnt. That is a function network marketing can perform indeed.

To get started with any type of business, you could opt to first go through an extensive (and expensive) education – but you will not be making any money while you are doing so. Network marketing makes it possible to start with relatively little money (commonly less than $3000) and to obtain the necessary education while you are building the business and while you are making your first money. This combination is unique – if you are looking for an opportunity like that, an honorable (!) network marketing company might be an option for you.

If you are looking for some kind of investment (throw money at it and pray) or some sort of gambling (like a lottery and the next hot stock tip), then network marketing organizations are the wrong place to look. If a network looks like a lottery, it for most part is a scam.

Network marketing is self-employment, which means: lots of work.

Whenever somebody tells you that you in essence have no work at all and everything is done for you or automated – run! This person wants only one thing, and that is your money.

"Lots of work" doesn't mean you have to slave away through the nights until you keel over or drop near-dead into your bed, though. Far away from it. Network marketing, more than any other type of business, allows you to organize your time and environment, and to meet in cheerful atmosphere for easy-going conversations with your prospects. You can work out their needs, wishes, and fears – and maybe offer a solution, if your network fits the bill. All that normally is going on in a private setting like living room, kitchen table, café, or restaurant.

Those benefits are well worth the effort of exposing yourself to these models. But none of these justifies blindly jumping into hazardous adventures with no chance for success, just because somebody promises double-digit returns.

Your investment should be mainly into your own education and business experience (real education, not academic) – the result you will be able to use almost anywhere you go, be it in this network, in another one or simply in a traditional hierarchical company. Network marketing can make an important contribution to this strategy, more than any other type of self-employment.

Realistically speaking, you can look at network marketing as a type of paid learning (i.e. you are being paid to learn). Still, it's not a magic wand.

Should you now have further questions regarding the content of this book, feel free to get in touch (in English language) via my Facebook page:

https://www.facebook.com/SRalfCarter/

About the Author

S. Ralf Carter is self-employed and business owner since more than 30 years; about half of this time, he has been performing diverse functions in the software industry.

Wherever there has been the opportunity to try wrong decisions, Ralf Carter most likely did try them or at least did experience live how business partners had to work through the consequences of their own suboptimal decisions.

During the second half of his career, he additionally provided (and still provides) his experience for the training of entrepreneurs and business start-ups.

Born in Germany, over time he has called several parts of the world his home. Right now, a sunny Mediterranean island is his residence of choice.

He writes as a network marketing insider, himself working with the company Jeunesse Global, where you can find his website

https://paphos.jeunesseglobal.com/

Glossary

Each area of our lives has its own slang and special terminology, which bears no relationship with anything else and which you don't need to know or understand as long as you don't want to interact with that specific area of specialty. For instance, the epic width of medical terminology is entirely irrelevant for an architect. The other way round applies as well.

For that reason, you may have encountered terms in this book at one place or another, which are not used in your current world or which appear to have a different meanings. I did try to avoid them, but in case something sneaked into the book – here are explanations of some of those terms.

B

Bitcoin

The probably oldest crypto currency. Has made some headlines recently, when the relatively low processing capacity of the Bitcoin computing net has lead to partially gigantic backlogs of pending transactions and has caused outrageously high transaction fees (to the magnitude of several hundred dollars for a transaction of barely more than 2000 dollar).

Those problems have highlighted the necessity of revamping the Bitcoin transaction systems, since without a major overhaul Bitcoin at this time seems totally unfit for use as a general payment system.

It's important to understand the difference between the Bitcoin currency and its transaction processing system – the two are essentially unrelated, just like the US dollar is not directly tied to the computer systems of a banking group.

Bitcoin as a currency faces some issues with the governments (no surprise here), which try to make taxation of Bitcoin transactions as unattractive as possible. Most European countries have slapped Bitcoin with the worse of both worlds (monetary instrument and non-financial asset). It's probably not far fetched to assume governments want to protect their own money and remove competition as good as possible without causing a revolution.

Blockchain

Public transaction log for crypto currencies like, for example, Bitcoin.

C

Capital

Access to money. Often used interchangeably with the term "money", but in many cases, loans can replace money – so, capital may be money or a loan (i.e. access to money)

Commission

Compensation paid for a service, usually related to referral services like salespeople, brokers and insurance agents

Compensation Plan, Compensation Model

A model or plan is a combined set of fixed rules, according to which something is supposed to be done. If those rules refer to calculating and paying commissions and other types of compensation, that's called a compensation plan. Other professions may call it a "fee model" or "remuneration plan"

Consumer Loan

Loan provided to consumers with the intention of stimulating sales of consumption items such as tv-sets, furniture or cars

Credit Card

Payment method with attached on-demand line of credit. The payment is performed from the line of credit made available by the issuing credit card bank. Credit cards provide a very easy-to-use type of loan, which should be paid off within a few days after you receive the billing statement – otherwise it will get very expensive very fast

Creditor

Essentially the same as a lender. Used with a slightly different connotation: a creditor may have provided anything worth money and expects to be paid with money, while a lender usually is a creditor who has provided money itself

Crypto Currency

Virtual "currency", which is issued and managed not by a central bank but by means of a (very time-consuming) mathematical mining algorithm. For most part, crypto currencies have maximum number of "coins" (integral units with only zeros after the decimal point), which makes them theoretically immune to any attempt to hyper-inflate.

Acceptance of crypto currencies is completely voluntary, tributes to the governments cannot be paid using crypto currencies at all; minor exceptions are some Swiss municipalities that do accept payment in Bitcoin, similarly the Swiss railway company and some prepaid phone refills/top-ups, also in Switzerland.

Common attribute of all crypto currencies is the public transaction log (called blockchain), where everybody can look up each individual transaction ever performed. Further, all crypto currencies are working decentrally: instead of using a central clearing house (such as a central bank as the ECB or the Fed), transaction are recorded by many (millions) different and independent computers – after-the-fact-falsifications are even less likely than with traditional banking; the blockchain most likely is significantly safer than traditional banking systems.

D

Deutschmark (DM)

(West) Germany's currency between 1948 and 2000/2001; was replaced in 2000 (for bank accounts) and 2001 (coins and notes) by the new Euro at an exchange rate of 1.95583 DM per Euro.

Direct Sales

A form of retail distribution based on a direct buyer-seller-relationship between the manufacturer/importer and the end-customer. In contrast to traditional wholesaler models (where the goods pass through several stages on their way from manufacturer to customer), direct sales models deliver the products directly from manufacturer to customer. Marketing and sales for direct sales models usually are performed by multi-level-marketing (MLM) organizations

Discount

A discount is a reduction of a payment to you, intended to account for the payor's risk of not knowing the future. Therefore, a discount always leads to a lower payment to you. Even if afterwards it becomes clear that the discount was not (or not fully) justified, the discount will not be adjusted retroactively.

Discounted

Description used for an amount, which has been reduced by a discount.

E

European Union (EU)

Collective term for the many different transnational European political organizations, which are increasingly pooling their bureaucratic system within a joint apparatus. For the purposes of this book the most important aspect is the fact that the member states of the EU have transferred many of their governmental powers to EU agencies, specifically in areas of health or financial regulation.

Therefore, pharmaceuticals (medications) can be registered once with the EU and then have permission to be sold anywhere in the EU (for most part). The same is true for the financial industry; banks by now are centrally regulated by the ECB (European Central Bank), while financial service providers are still supervised by individual countries' agencies – but within the common legal framework.

Also, asset freezes and arrest warrants are executed EU-wide, regardless of which country the original issue came from. That's the reason why fraudsters by now have to live and bank outside the EU to be safely outside legal reach (instead of previously banking in the Czech Republic or Luxembourg).

In effect, despite not being a nation state, the European Union shares many of the hallmarks of a federal nation state like the USA.

The EU borders in this context come as a surprise for many people: England and Wales despite Brexit still belong to the EU, while the British Channel Islands do not (British crown territories). The micro-states of Malta and Cyprus are part of the EU, while Gibraltar (geographically attached to Spain) is not. Sweden is part of the EU, Norway is not. Switzerland is part of the European Economic Area (EEA) but not part of the EU, while the Caribbean island Bonaire does belong to the EU (as county of the Netherlands). Turkey doesn't belong to the EU, nor does Iceland; the Dutch part of the Caribbean island St. Martin is also not part of the EU, while the French part of the same island is. Contrary to popular belief, Bavaria still belongs to Germany and therefore to the European Union.

Euro (EUR)

Common currency of the European Union. The contracts stipulated joining the common currency as long-term requirement for every EU-country. However, it appears as if joining has become optional rather than a requirement.

The Euro is issued and managed by the European Central Bank (ECB) in Frankfurt, Germany.

Faltin, Günter

German professor (FU Berlin) and entrepreneur (Tee-Kampagne); known to re-think existing business models and turn traditional structures upside down

Financial Service Provider

In most countries, the business with client deposits (for purpose of handling those monies) is heavily regulated and reserved for special institutions. Basic requirements are intense supervision of the internals and extensive capital. Such institutions are commonly banks, savings banks, credit unions (in the US) or building societies (in the UK).

Aside from those core financial companies, there are adjacent areas where companies are not acting as deposit holders, but are providing services related to the core financial industry. Those areas are called financial services, the companies providing them consequently are financial service providers.

Such services are the sales and promotion of investments (unless classified as bank service anyway), execution of financial transactions outside the banking business (credit card payments, online payment systems, currency exchanges as often found in airports), referral of insurance contracts, transacting stock or bond orders on behalf of customers (those services are provided by brokers or banks).

Financial Service Providers themselves are subject to supervision and regulation by each country's respective authority.

HMRC

Her Majesty's Revenue and Customs; the British governmental department charged with collecting taxes and customs

Inc.

Abbreviation for „Incorporated". In many jurisdiction a permitted indication for a legal structure with limited liability

Initiator

To start a project of any kind and raise money from investors, somebody needs to take on the job of organizing everything involved. This somebody is called the initiator. The initiator is not necessarily the person with the original idea (actually, rarely is) but somebody who is capable in the area of project management and has a very good working knowledge of applicable laws and common usances in the financial industry.

Among the many tasks for initiators are creation of sales prospectuses for the investments, checking the management's cash flow forecasts, legal evaluations of the project environment and so on.

In practice, as it turns out, the initiator oftentimes is exactly the one who wrote the forecasts, to begin with – therefore, that person is checking its own documents for viability; hardly a confidence-instilling situation

Installment Loans

A type of loan for which the loan contract right from the beginning stipulates the due dates and amounts of the payments to be made by the borrower

Insurance Agent

A salesperson for insurance contracts, frequently limited to offers from just one insurance conglomerate (despite featuring different brand names)

Interests

Time cost of capital. Usually are charged on day granularity, means: you keep the capital one day longer, you pay interests for one more day.

Installment loans (including their specialized version mortgage loans) usually have a blockage against premature repayment; while the bank is happily accepting your payment, premature payments will **not** be credited against the amount owed. Instead, the bank keeps the money in a separate account and credits the amounts to your loan only on the respective due dates. In these cases, paying off the loan early does not provide a benefit.

In all other cases, especially revolving loans like credit card loans or lines of credit, every day you don't use the loan (i.e. pay it off earlier) will lead to lower interest costs

Investigative Journalism

A frequently over-sensational representation of facts or circumstances. After cutting out the artifical pressures on tear or ephedrine glands, often barely more is left but facts which were previously known or could have obtained by mere thinking

Investment

A vehicle to participate in somebody else's projects. To qualify as an investment, the project frequently had to be packed and repackaged to a point where it appears quasi sterile to the investor and at which point the investor doesn't have any work or concern with the project. Those aspects are left to others, which provide those tasks for a free – and who are shielding you against the fallout of the day-to-day operations, such as legal affairs.

This multi-layer-repackaging is intended for the investor's protection, but even more so for protection of the project and the project's management. If such investment generates a large profit over time, it happened quasi accidentally and has not been intended or planned for.

Over time, the term investment has become synonymous with a purchase of shares in a mutual fund corporation (which itself is heavily regulated)

IRS

Internal Revenue Service – the US agency charged with collecting federal taxes in the United States of America

---

J

Jurisdiction

Regional legal framework, normally consider "the law" by people living in that region. However, in times of transregional and international business, "the law" has become a quite useless reference – what's required in one place may be illegal in another.

While civil law is surprisingly uniform in Western countries, criminal law is more diverse – and tax law is a total mess. In the US, sales tax rates differ from city to city and county to county as much as the goods subjected to it are different. Canada doesn't even have a sales tax but a GST, which follows an entirely different regimen. The US state of Louisiana has a sales tax, but its procedures are closer to a European-style VAT than to the sales tax of its US neighbors.

When referring to "jurisdiction", all levels of jurisdictions need to be taken into account: municipality (city), small regional (county, parish), larger region (US state, Canadian province) and national entity (USA, Canada, UK) and potentially supranational bodies like NAFTA or the EU.

L

Lender

Somebody who lends you money and believes you are able and willing to pay money and interests back. Common lenders are banks, insurances, credit unions and your relatives.

Caused by a weird idiosyncracy, our brains tend to confront a financial crisis (i.e. when we are unable to repay) by blaming the lender for our problems. We come up with strange reasonings for this conclusion – such as the lenders being at fault because they should have known that we are unable to repay (despite ourselves having done everything in our power to make the lender believe we could pay in the future!).

This ridiculous behavior has been cultivated by kings and states in past times because, thanks to their military, they saw the option to bedevil the lenders and therafter purge these devils from within mankind – and to escape their repayment obligations this way.

Apparently, modern humans seem to ignore the fact that we do not own an army we could throw against our lenders; an exception may be the US of A, which indeed have a large enough army and large enough debt to make it worthwhile.

Limited

Refers to limited liability; in many jurisdictions, this is a permissible indication of a legal structure with limited liability (such as a corporation). In Britain and many countries of the British Commonwealth, the two forms of limited liability companies are named "Ltd." (for privately held corporations) and "plc" (for stock-exchange-listed or -listable corporations).

Limited Liability

In business, one of the main issues is the question of who is liable for what. Unless you go through special efforts, you are liable for all debts and damages caused by your business – which can ruin your finances for essentially the rest of your life.

Essentially all jurisdiction allow to set up special legal structures limiting liability to only the assets owned by that legal entity; essentially, by act of government, this entity is granted its own legal life.

As long as managers and owners of that entity behave in a lawful manner and are trying to anticipate all potential risks, this limited liability entity shields them against claims from the outside.

This so-called corporate shield or veil doesn't protect against the consequences of illegal activities, consequences of predictable failure and intentional damage.

Typical entities with limited liability are Corp (corporation), LLC (limited liability company) and Inc (corporation) in the US, Ltd (Limited) and PLC (public limited company) in the UK, AG (corporation) and GmbH (limited liability company) in Germany, Switzerland and Austria, as well as SA (corporation) and SRL/SARL (limited liability company) in French- and Spanish-speaking juristictions

Limited Partnership

Semi-legal structure used for business purposes. Has at least 2 owners, one of which provides unlimited liability and manages the company; the other partner contributes capital, but the liability is limited to the contribution. The limited partner does not manage the business

Line of Credit

An on-demand loan, provided by your bank. Flexibel and very easy to use (you just withdraw from the loan account or write a check against it), but also the most problematic and most expensive form of credit: your bank can change availability, terms and interest rate at the blink of an eye

Loan

A contract between a lender (often a bank) and another person (for example you), called the borrower, under which the lender gives the borrower money for a certain time in exchange for the promise to repay the money plus a fee (called interests) for using the money during that time

Ltd.

Abbreviation of "Limited"; refers to a legal structure with limited liability and is in many jurisdiction a permissible indication of such legal entity

Margin

The difference between two amounts. For margins in the context of brokerage, see margin loan.

For retail businesses, the margin refers to the gross profits of the goods sold, often considered to be the difference between retail price and wholesale price. This interpretation falls a bit short, though – the margin needs to be reduced by shipping costs and, where applicable, the VAT (value added taxes). Further reductions are caused by price discounts (for example after-the-fact price reductions if the merchandise was of poor quality), finance costs and other costs directly attributable to the goods sold.

The margin can be expressed as an amount (e.g. $3.50 per pack) or as a percentage. Or as a share of the moon phase, but that wouldn't make much sense

Margin Loan

A dynamic line of credit provided by your stock or bond broker. This line of credit is secured by your stock or bond portfolio and is frequently monitored on at least daily basis, more likely every minute. Should the market value of your portfolio fall below the critical threshold, the broker can start selling your securities to cover the shortfall – and often does so without much of a prewarning. The obvious problem is the continuously fluctuating stock price, which leads to fluctuation values of your collateral.

On top of that, not only your broker can change collateral requirements, but the central bank can do the same; if the central bank makes those changes, it affects all margin loan clients – but I doubt it's much of a consolation to know that you are not the only one going bust

Mass Media

TV, radio, or newspapers aimed at a very large number of people. In general, aimed at nobody in particular and therefore in need to gain attention by using most outrageous headlines and claims ridiculous beyond belief

MLM

Abbreviation for Multi-Level-Marketing

Mortgage loan

A commonly long-running installment loan (often 10 to 30 years), secured by tentative transfer of ownership in real estate (the so-called mortgage). If you do not live up to your payment obligations under the loan contract, the lender (usually a bank) has the right to liquidate the collateral – means: to take away the property and sell it with the help of the legal system. Should the sales proceeds fail to cover the loan, the remaining debt still remains you responsibility. However, in some jurisdictions the lender is not permitted to seize any other asset. That doesn't prevent the lender from blemishing your credit report, though.

Multi-Level-Marketing

Similar to the term network marketing; used interchangeably in this book.

The term "multi-level-marketing" emphasizes that marketing is spread over several different levels and that commissions are following this spread-out approach.

Unfortunately, a common misconception interprets the "multi-level" as referring to the flow of products and invoicing, assuming each level adds to the product price. This definitely does not apply, but instead is a basic property of what most people would consider a "proper business" model, the wholesaler-retailer-model. Due to this misunderstanding, the inherent disadvantage of its main opponent is ascribed to MLM, wrongly so.

Instead, MLM is a marketing form for direct sales

Mutual Funds

A corporation with variable capital (as opposed to normal corporations which have a fixed capital base); heavily regulated, set up for the purpose of pooling investments from a large number of people.

Despite many differences in mutual funds regulations between different jurisdictions, the one common denominator is: this is a legal structure intended to be setup by banks; therefore, if you do anything remotely resembling a mutual funds, expect legal problems and crossfire from banks

Network Marketing

A form of sales and marketing, based on many self-employed persons and relying on word-of-mouth and recommendations from existing customers. Similar and partially identical terms are multi-level-marketing, MLM and direct sales.

Payroll Taxes

An amount kept by the employer and forwarded to the government. Depending on the jurisdiction, the payroll tax may include an advance payment for your personal income tax, a contribution to old-age pension schemes, unemployment insurance, health insurance, and others.

Also quite common, the employee pays "half" of the payroll tax, the other half is forked over by the employer. This "sharing" is a gambler's slide of hand because the only source an employer could use to pay for those taxes happens to be the labor of the employee – which simply means the employee pays for everything, the governments just don't want to openly admit how much they took.

In many countries (verified for the UK, US, Germany) the payroll tax withholding can be adjusted by the taxpayer/employee if he is reasonably expecting losses from a business startup – that way, the taxpayer can start a business with before-taxes-cash rather than with cash left-over after taxes

Professionals

For the context of this book, a professional is somebody who normally would be classified as a commercial self-employed person – but by virtue of law is defined as non-commercial. Depending on the jurisdiction, the list of professions differs; in most cases, though, you can find professions like lawyers, doctors, accountants, economists, teachers and artists as well as writers and midwives on those lists.

Mostly, those professionals benefit from a more advantageous tax regimen than do other self-employed persons.

In many countries, a professional is not permitted to do anything which is not on that list of professions – which is why, in many cases, attorneys and doctors are not very responsive to network marketing efforts simply because they are not allowed to. But their spouses frequently are open to commercial ideas (as which network marketing would qualify)

R

Robber Barons of Revenue Castle

Employees of the departments of revenue (IRS, FTB, HMRC,...)

The phrase derives from a term coined by the German tax book author Franz Konz (deceased 2013) who equated the revenue employees to robber barons of Medieval Europe, hiding in their castles behind strong walls which protected them against the fallout of their actions

Saving

Accumulation of money in a specifically dedicated location, usually a savings account with a bank. In times of high costs of capital, bank and credit unions are trying to attract customers' savings to lower their own costs of capital. As incentive, the banks offer a small interest payment to make their institution more attractive for saver's money.

Over time, people's perceiption has shifted from the original purpose of savings (adding up small amounts to become a larger one) to the idea of replacing self-responsible investments. Savings accounts cannot provide this investment function, which led many people to consider savings outdated and old-fashioned

Self-Employed

Somebody who performs activities repeatedly and with profit intent. Usually the term refers to commercial self-employed persons; for non-commercial self-employeds, commonly the term "Professional" is used.

In most jurisdictions, self-employed persons need some kind of business license, which for most activities is simply a registration. For a few (or not so few) activities, the self-employed will need a permit – that's especially true if the self-employed is qualified as professional. However, in areas like real estate, finance and medical profession, almost everywhere special permits are required

Sole Proprietorship

Legal structure for a business owner in case there is no legal structure. This term is used as a handle or replacement for cases when there is no legal structure that could be named. Example:

"Is your business incorporated?"

"No, I am in business by myself, just me, no entity"

"So you are operating a sole proprietorship"

Taxes

Involuntary tributes without discernible marketing efforts, to be paid to governments. Occasionally, the lack of proper marketing for taxes leads to public unrest or upset, which is when politicians come up with vague fantasy terms as explanation, which have nothing to do with the tax nor its justification – but those attempts frequently are accepted by the minds of taxpayers as "good enough", leading to further payment of the tax.

Typical phrases used in these contexts are psycho-triggers like "tax evasion", "tax loophole", "fair share of the burden" or "tax subsidy" (interesting shift for the semantics of "subsidy" – away from "paying to" towards "not receiving from")

TFM

Time for money

Tributes

Amounts collected by a ruler or government from its underlings. While politicians and bureaucracies differentiate between tributes with presumed justification (usually called contributions, prefixed by an entirely unrelated word, such as "social security contribution" which is neither social nor secure) and tributes without justification (called taxes), this differentiation is purely an outflow of marketing aspects, therefore this book treats them as interchangeable.

The governments themselves see it exactly the way this book does: whenever one pot of money dries up for any reason, the governments use the funds from the other source as if the were interchangeable and just synonymous. Which means: they are.

Woolmilkpork

Expression used for what a person wants in case of unreasonable
demands. Based on the idea of demanding wool, milk and pork from
the same animal. It's essentially a noun for the request to "have
your cake and eat it, too"